ENTERPRISE RESOURCE PLANNING

Concepts and Practice

SECOND EDITION

Vinod Kumar Garg

Formerly Professor of Information Management

S.P. Jain Institute of Management and Research

Mumbai

and

N.K. Venkitakrishnan

Co-Founder and Director

SATTRIX Information Security Private Limited

Mumbai

PHI Learning Private Limited

Delhi-110092

2026

*In fond memory of **Shri Asoke K. Ghosh** (October 1942 – February 2024), Founder Chairman and Managing Director of PHI Learning, whose vision endlessly inspires.*

The Legacy Continues....

Published by Pushpita Ghosh, PHI Learning Private Limited, Rimjhim House, 111, Patparganj Industrial Estate, Delhi-110092 and Printed by Gopsons Printers Pvt. Ltd., A-14, Sector-60, Noida, Gautambudh Nagar, Noida, Uttar Pradesh-201301.

₹525.00

ENTERPRISE RESOURCE PLANNING—Concepts and Practice, 2nd ed.
Vinod Kumar Garg and N.K. Venkitakrishnan

ISBN-978-81-203-2254-7 (Print Book)
ISBN-978-93-5443-002-2 (e-Book)

To the all pervading
Lord Krishna

निमित्तमात्रं भव सव्यसाचिन्

Contents

Preface

In this edition, we have tried to highlight the Indian ERP Packages, by inserting a section on "Example of an Indian ERP Package" that includes the integrated features of the ERP and explains the ERP III Architecture in brief. Also, two case studies have been inserted in Chapter 8, which demonstrate the successful implementation of the ERP package in India.

It has been an ongoing demand from the academic community that this book should have exercise problems at the end of chapters to make it a complete textbook. To this effect, we had added about 25 problems that cover most of the topics in the book. To help the academic community further, in the Second Edition we have provided hints and clues to most of these questions. However, these are only to be taken as guidelines.

We fervently hope that these additions and changes will make the text more useful and reader friendly.

Vinod Kumar Garg
N.K. Venkitakrishnan

Preface to the First Edition

Today, national economies are undergoing rapid and substantial transformation. Two forces underlie such changes. One is globalization—the explosive growth of global trade and international competition. No country can isolate itself from the world economy. If it closes its markets to foreign competition, its citizens may pay much more for lower quality goods. The other force is technological change. This decade has witnessed remarkable advances in the availability of information and speed of communication. Everyday, newer products are being offered, particularly in the electronic goods sector.

In addition to globalization and technological change, we are witnessing a power shift from manufacturers to giant retailers and growing consumer price and value sensitivity. These changes are throwing companies into a state of confusion regarding strategy. They have to protect their profits and remain competitive in a crowded market which is characterized by unprecedented competitive pressures and sophisticated customers. All these demand speedy solutions. Companies have to primarily respond by being cost competitive and, more essentially, reengineer their business processes.

With the emergence of powerful personal computers and the success of the Internet, consumers need no longer wait for business to lock them into any proprietary technology. The advent of the client/server concept has made remarkable differences in the approach of a customer in deciding a solution of his or her need and choice. Finally, the core aspect of process orientation in business and implementation of these aspects to achieve competitive advantage can be realized only by accepting the concept of Enterprise Resource Planning (ERP).

This book is intended for the wide spectrum of readers who wish to understand the concepts underlying ERP. For the managers it provides an in-depth, clear understanding of business processes and how ERP helps in reengineering these processes. The book also provides a comprehensive reference for ERP and has broad application for business, consultants and academia.

For business leaders—either those already involved in business or about to be involved in new business design and ERP implementation, this book will help address the various issues of implementing an ERP solution while at the same time allay their fears of switching over from the current system to a more business oriented solution.

This book is intended to equip business decision makers, consultants, and students to manage more effectively areas that are strategic to successfully run information technology oriented companies. It is expected to provide a deep understanding of the need for implementing an ERP solution of the real issues of business that provide value to customers and enable the managerial personnel to maintain a competitive edge and tackle real-life solutions more effectively and on time.

Vinod Kumar Garg
N.K. Venkitakrishnan

Acknowledgements

Any book of this kind relies primarily on the studies of authentic business situations and on articles published in various computer journals and magazines. We had to depend on such information and the feedback sent by various organizations that have implemented ERP. We wish to acknowledge all such assistance. Our deep appreciation is also due to numerous business managers and executives who have so generously given their time and advice which was based on their experience of encountering various day-to-day business problems and how an ERP implementation solution has provided a respite.

We also wish to express our sincere appreciation to Dr. A.K. Chitale of GS Institute of Technology & Science, Indore and Dr. V.N. Garg of IITM, Indore, who helped us in taking the initial decision to prepare this book for publication. Similarly, we acknowledge with gratitude the support and encouragement of our colleagues at CyberTech Systems and Software Limited.

We profusely thank Narendra Nadkar, Lata Chablani and Reshmi Nair of CyberTech Systems and Software Limited for their assistance in the preparation of the manuscript.

We would like to specially mention Sarita Garg, Neeti Garg, Vikram Garg, Uma Venkitakrishnan and Vasudha Venkitakrishnan for all the encouragement, patience and special care shown by them so that we could successfully complete the manuscript on time.

We are also grateful to our parents Dr. R.P. Garg, Kailashi Garg, N.V. Kailasam, Lakshmi Kailasam and all our family members for their constant blessing and guidance, without which this publication would not have been possible.

Finally, we would like to express our sincere thanks to the publishers, PHI Learning whose encouragement and assistance have helped in the speedy and quality publication of the book.

Vinod Kumar Garg
N.K. Venkitakrishnan

Prologue

Market Overview

Today, many organizations face continuous demands from rapidly changing and increasingly competitive global markets. They also must serve customers who want innovative, high-quality products that feature special options. Additionally, further pressures are created by technology developments that shorten many product life cycles, and by intensified international competition which drives corporations to reduce costs and improve production efficiencies.

To increase their competitive advantage, companies must have flexible business information systems that adapt to rapid changes. To address these needs, enterprise business applications must provide solutions that concentrate on the customer by integrating the supply chain.

Enterprise Resource Planning (ERP) is one of the fastest growing segments of Information Technology today. Though numerous articles and reports keep appearing in computer magazines and newspapers, the information is not available in consolidated form. This book *ERP—Concepts and Practice* is an attempt to fill this lacuna and is, therefore, expected to be of assistance to students and practitioners alike.

1

ERP—A Curtain Raiser

An Overview

The business environment has changed more in the last five years than it did over the previous five decades. The pace of change continues to accelerate and corporations around the world seek to revitalize, reinvent and resize in an effort to position themselves for success in the 21st century. The ability to respond to new customer needs and seize market opportunities as they arise is crucial. Successful companies today recognize that a high level of interaction and coordination along the supply chain will be a key ingredient of their continued success. Enterprises are continuously striving to improve themselves in the areas of quality, time to market, customer satisfaction, performance and profitability. Tomorrow's winners will be those businesses that can most effectively gather, and quickly act upon crucial information. Making informed business decisions in this manner would enable organizations to accomplish their business growth and at the same time enable them to utilize the information to competitive advantage.

To make it possible for the companies to execute this vision, there is a need for an infrastructure that will provide information across all functions and locations within the organization. The Enterprise Resource Planning (ERP) software fulfils this need.

This chapter gives an overview of ERP, its scope, benefits and its evolution.

Companies, public or private, whether in the manufacturing or the service sector, have always been searching for the "total solution". MRP II, the closed-loop manufacturing resources planning which used to be the panacea for all enterprise resource planning problems not as long ago, has now become only a subset of this overall objective. Today, the entire enterprise must be managed within a more global, tightly integrated, closed-loop solution. This expanded functionality can be called **Enterprise Resources Planning (ERP)**. Figure 1.1 represents this concept of enterprise resources planning and execution, symbolizing integrated functionality and the global nature of today's enterprises. The figure is assumed to consist of four quadrants, the circle at its centre represents the entities that constitute the central database shared by all functions of the enterprise while the border represents the cross-enterprise functionality that must be shared by all systems.

ACCOMMODATING VARIETY

The most important part of this cross-enterprise border will be known as **"multi'**, representing the capability required by it to compete and succeed globally. Today's total software solution must provide both multilingual and **multi-currency** capabilities, and be flexible enough to have customer service representatives in different countries taking orders in different languages and at the same time on a single host platform. Orders must be printed or returned to customers in their native languages. **Multi-currency** functionality must be capable of, for instance, receiving invoices in Indian Rupees, splitting the payment into German Marks and Belgian Francs, billing in Italian Lire, receiving cash in British Pounds, with the general ledger stated in US Dollars or Japanese Yen.

Another critical multi is **multi-mode** or **mixed-mode manufacturing.** In the enterprise of today, grown through alliance and merger, a single manufacturing strategy of either discrete or continuous process is no longer practical. Enterprises now employ a mix of approaches including make-to-stock, highly-repetitive, assemble-to-order or design-to-order. A single integrated software solution, and not satellite software, should handle all these concurrently, efficiently passing data from one to the other.

Another significant multi is **multi-facility.** The total solution must support multiple divisions or companies under a corporate banner. Multiple facilities are logical or physical entities linked to divisions. Each of these may or may not have independent stores, production units, assembly lines, overhead centres, and planning units but each usually has a set of accounts. Each and every transaction must flow seamlessly to the divisions' or corporate's set of books. The software should also seamlessly integrate operating platforms as the corporate database and departmental level applications may be required to run on a variety of hardware and software platforms.

INTEGRATED MANAGEMENT INFORMATION

Today's users require flexible reporting tools to extract the information as

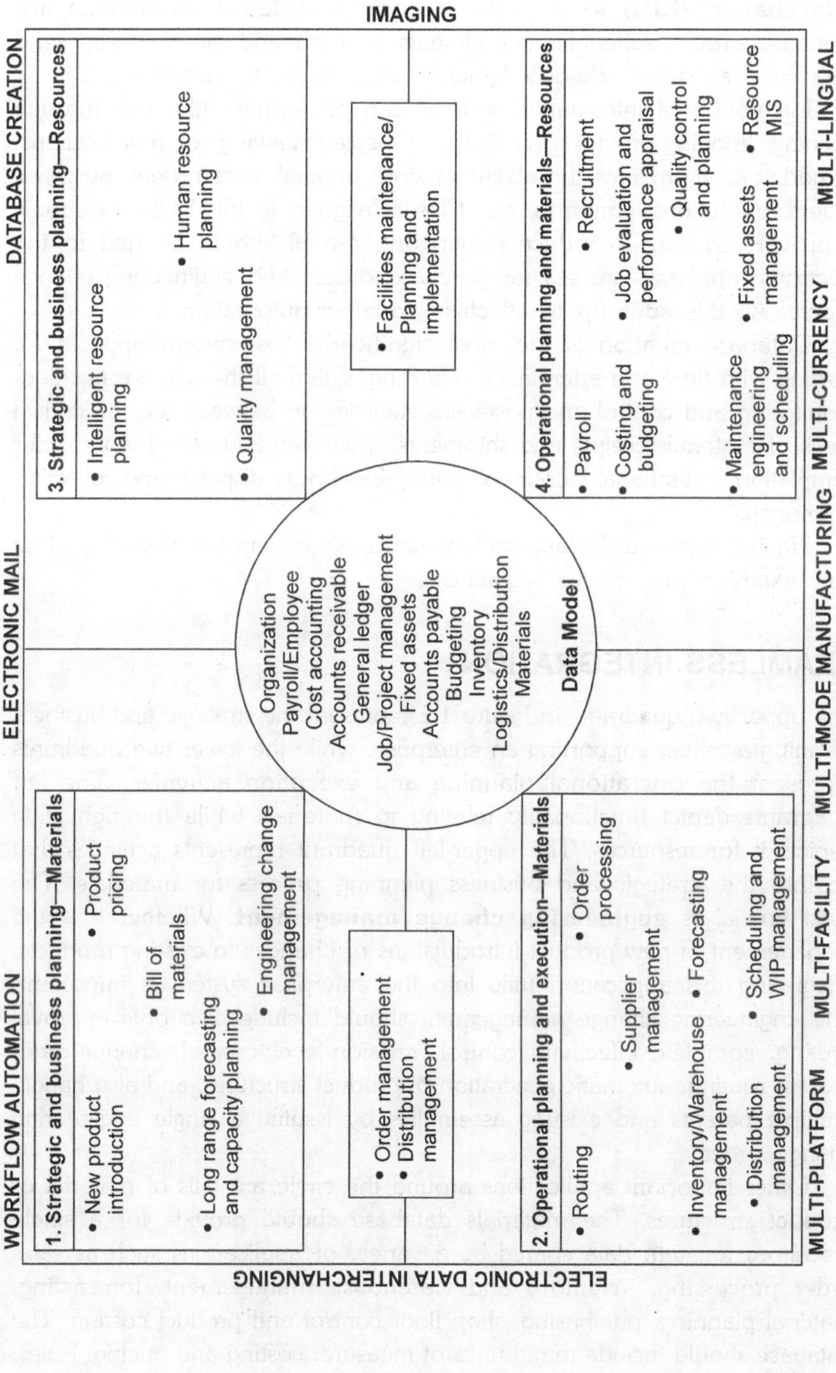

Fig. 1.1 General model for ERP.

and when they need it without depending on an information systems department to produce the report. And they also need **electronic data interchange (EDI)** to electronically accept customer information like purchase orders, schedule amendments or cash and electronically send data such as order acknowledgment and invoices to customers.

Integration of information systems can be further enhanced through imaging. Imaging provides the ability to display drawings or specifications. In addition, it provides the ability to store original sales orders, purchase orders, quotations, contracts, etc. Closely aligned to this is the electronic approval process. To reduce paperwork, e-mail should be tied to the electronic approval process for purchase orders and engineering change orders. All this adds up to effective workflow automation.

Database creation is the most significant cross-system application, starting with time and attendance reporting, going all the way to machine-monitoring and control and post-sales statistics. In between are the critical areas of material receipts and shipments, inventory issues and work order completion, operational labour collection, warehouse dispatch and collection of money.

Having explored the applications and cross-system functionality, let us now examine the various segments.

SEAMLESS INTEGRATION

The upper two quadrants in Figure 1.1 represent the strategic and business planning activities supporting an enterprise, while the lower two quadrants represent the operational planning and execution activities. The left quadrants depict functionality relating to materials while the right side depicts it for resources. The upper-left quadrant represents activities that go into the strategic and business planning process for materials. The most crucial is **engineering change management.** Whether it is the management of new product introductions or changes to existing products, integrating this application fully into the enterprise system is important. The engineering change management should include electronic approval routing, complete effectivity control, revision-level control, change-order process routing, automatic generation of product structures, and also handle multiple parents and existing assemblies by issuing a single engineering change order.

Other important applications around the circle are bills of material or product structures. The materials database should provide for a single repository for item data shared by a variety of applications such as sales order processing, inventory and warehouse management, forecasting, material planning, purchasing, shop floor control and product costing. The database should include many units of measure, costing and pricing. Rules, and multiple item numbers per item with full cross-referencing capabilities are specific functions that should be available along with provision for multiple locations where an item could be stored.

Product pricing for material should handle all necessary cost information like direct material cost as well as the kind of cost, from last in, weighted average, or predicted value at its source. It should add overhead costs such as costs related to quality control, research and development, utilities, warehouse movement and space, scrap, or outside processing. It should also provide for various pricing scenarios and their impact on performance parameters such as sales and profitability. Interactive inquiries and reports should be available to display this information.

The strategic planning and operations application concerning materials is integrated by order management and distribution management. Specific line items within one order should be able to be directed to individual shipping points preferably with the help of electronic data interchange

The lower-left quadrant relates to applications involving execution of the materials function. It should be possible to do the most important forecasting at various levels, for example, the item and/or aggregate level, and the system should be able to select a suitable forecasting method based on data. Multiple forecasts should be available to represent geographic regions, time periods, market segments and business units, on request.

The other applications include distribution management, scheduling, routing and **work-in-progress (WIP)** management. The applications in the lower-left quadrant should be integrated allowing a seamless flow from one application to the other. The functionality provided should support timing, planning periods, type of items included or excluded, changes in safety stock and re-order policies.

SUPPLY CHAIN MANAGEMENT

End-to-end supply chain management is increasingly becoming crucial as many of today's enterprises are a complex mixture of manufacturing/ distribution sites, multiple manufacturing sites and/or distribution networks. Hence, a method to optimize the overall flow of demand and supply data must be present. This is known as **intelligent resource planning (IRP).** IRP allows an enterprise to build relationships between various activities to optimally identify the demand supply chain. It should include interplant order processing, availability checking and cost optimization. IRP should also support creation of alternate scenarios in terms of resource utilization and delivery performance.

The other applications in the left quadrant are directed at the execution rather than the planning aspects of materials. Supplier management is becoming important in view of globalization. In addition to normal purchasing functionality, vendor release scheduling, variable receipts routing on a vendor-by-item combination and complete vendor analysis must also be provided.

One of the crucial aspects of supply chain management is inventory management that must allow flexibility in how inventory is located, stored and controlled by providing for multiple locations and levels. Warehouse management should provide system-directed movements based on user-defined parameters, to maximize space utilization, personnel productivity, and delivery schedules. Additional functionality should include transportation planning, load planning and consolidation, as well as carrier and route selection. Import/export management controls, letter of credit processing and manifest and bill of lading processing, as well as export documentation on a country-by-country basis should be fully linked to EDI transactions.

Scheduling and WIP management is another key operations application. Rate-based scheduling is critical in highly repetitive situations. Using these applications dispenses with formal work orders and substitutes a daily, weekly or monthly schedule on an item-by-work centre basis. Reporting is greatly simplified, and when done properly, both conventional work orders and rate-based production could exist within the same work centre.

The traditional shop floor control still guides the majority of manufacturing enterprises. Work centre dispatching, shortage reporting, material and labour movement, as well as WIP activity, all need to be accommodated. Integration to sales order entry and job cost functions are critical to efficient cost control and customer satisfaction.

Finite scheduling provides the ability to constrain the load placed on a work centre through user-defined rules. Available hours, product dependencies and setup costs all need to be accounted for when finite planning is done. Tooling or operator skills could also be constraints relative to the creation of a schedule. The application needs to be interactive, allowing for many "what if" simulations.

RESOURCE MANAGEMENT

Two of the major resources that should be optimally planned are human resources and equipment. The upper-right quadrant represents the strategic and business planning centred on an enterprise's resources. Looking at human resources management, the functionality provided here should include the employee database, job descriptions and evaluations, applicant tracking, requisition management, performance review, cost benefits, career and succession planning, creating alternate organization structures, apart from taking care of the training needs of employees on a continuous basis.

Equipment is another critical resource. Online records need to be kept of equipment location and status. Proper accounting methods need to be followed in respect of equipment location to track unit, status, operating and maintenance costs. Time-accounting and billing must be integrated when the equipment is directly charged to a job.

There is a need to simulate equipment scheduling under various scenarios as generated by forecasting. The simulation should generate cost patterns including not only the costing for labour and material but should also include machine-run cost, setup cost, and fixed and variable overheads for both labour and machines. Extra costs should be allowed for as a percentage of value-added or total labour. Lastly, there should be provision for labour cost to be shown as standard, current, projected, or on any other user-defined basis.

The next strategic application area concerning resources is **total quality management (TQM).** This should include provision for quality planning required for ISO 9000 certification. The strategic execution applications are joined together by a facilities maintenance management application. Maintenance management is critical in that it must provide a "bridge" between the materials planning and maintenance planning functions, allowing planners from both sides to communicate with each other.

The last quadrant represents the operational planning and execution applications specific to resources. The most vital application is resource MIS. Resource MIS is driven from a forecast and should work out resource requirements for various periods, locations and their financial implications. It should be linked to capacity planning. Resource MIS should take the generated plans and spread them into work centres to analyze bottleneck areas or over-committed resources.

Time and attendance reporting needs to be integrated into the resource control system. Usually handled through the data collection applications, it needs to provide interfaces to time clocks through bar coding or key entry applications and should eventually be linked to payroll, job evaluation and performance appraisal.

Another important resource execution application is quality control. It provides the ability to monitor and track specifications regarding a product or process. It controls resources by identifying which equipment is required to execute the testing process, and how it is to be accomplished. Results gathered from the testing process need to be stored at the item level, allowing certificates of acceptance to be produced.

Manufacturing cost accounting provides for the tracking and analysis of costs directly related to the production process. Movements into and out of WIP, labour efficiency, material utilization, and actual-to-engineered variances all need to be tracked. This application literally lives within shop floor control, product data management and the general accounting ledgers.

A fixed asset management application should support multiple depreciation methods, disposal analysis, and responsibility reporting, financing and insurance information, in addition to property tax and license renewal information.

Budgeting provides the functionality to monitor performance to plan. It displays all the accumulated activity throughout the development, sales, manufacturing and distribution cycle against the planned numbers. Budgets should be available online for work centres, departments, divisions or companies.

The payroll application should not only provide for wage administration, step progression, billings and retroactive pay, but should also provide history and turnover analyses, full integration to accounts payable, and simple maintenance and mass change capability.

INTEGRATED DATA MODEL

The heart of any ERP exercise is the creation of an integrated data model. As discussed earlier, the application should provide the true integration capability over the entire enterprise system particularly providing for data for employees, suppliers and customers. The database should reflect transactions involving processing of purchase orders and engineering changes.

General accounting should provide for multiple ledgers and sub-ledgers on a division-by-division basis. Online management summaries and consolidation eliminate extensive paperwork handling. The ability to drill down through successive levels of data should be provided.

Data pertaining to job or project management is critical to many enterprises. Some firms may want to track the engineering, subcontracting, direct manufacturing and installation costs against a particular quoted job. It should also include the cost of a capital improvement project. It should be possible for older jobs and budgets to be copied into new ones.

Taken in its entirety, this enterprise resource planning and execution model and its flexible set of integrated applications will keep your operations flowing efficiently. If properly executed, it allows the enterprise to grow and flex, without the necessity of changing software solutions. It should be looked upon as the acquisition of an asset, not as an expenditure.

SCOPE

The various areas normally covered under the concept of ERP are:

Financials. Financial accounting, treasury management, enterprise control, and asset management.

Logistics. Production planning, materials management, plant maintenance, quality management, project systems, sales and distribution.

Human resources. Personnel management, training and development, skills inventory.

Workflow. Workflow integrates the entire organization with flexible assignment of tasks and responsibilities to locations, positions, jobs, groups, or individuals. It integrates every employee in the 'value chain' by providing a **versatile inbox (universal inbox)** at his or her workplace, which can be configured individually.

TECHNOLOGY

With technology making such rapid strides, companies have to frequently change their application systems due to technology obsolescence. Investment made in proprietary hardware and operating system has to be replaced with fresh investment in open systems.

With the emergence of client/server architecture, companies were able to extend the computing power to the end user and scale their investments in the central servers over a period of time. Since ERP vendors are servicing a large number of clients in a number of industries they can make a sizeable investment amount in R & D activities. Some of the companies invest millions of dollars and are closely involved in the latest technological advancements and hence are able to exploit the technology for business benefits.

BENEFITS OF ERP

Integrated, uniform, relevant, and up-to-date information is vital for the very existence of an enterprise. It gives the power to the right person to make decisions at the right time. This is only possible when the entire organization shares the same information and views it in the same perspective. Lack of integration affects other flows like men, machines and money.

ERP brings together people who work on shared tasks within the same enterprise or in their dealings with suppliers and customers. Enterprises have to ensure a smoother flow of information at all levels and between all parts of their organization; to access up-to-date information. Workflow integrates business processes. Some of the tangible benefits reported by industry are:

- Reduction of lead time by 60 per cent
- 99 per cent on-time shipments
- Doubled business

- Increase of inventory turns to over 30 per cent
- Cycle time cut to 80 per cent
- WIP reduced to 70 per cent.

Apart from these tangible benefits, there are intangible benefits like:

- Better customer satisfaction
- Improved vendor performance
- Increased flexibility
- Reduced quality costs
- Improved resource utility
- Improved information accuracy
- Improved decision-making capability.

Traditionally it has been manufacturing enterprises that are looking to improve efficiency, lower costs and increase profitability. The manufacturing industries that have successfully implemented ERP are in the automotive, discrete, consumer goods, chemical and pharmaceutical sectors. Other diverse enterprises such as banking and insurance, health care, telecom and utilities have also been quick to realize that ERP is a beneficial package for solving their problems also. These enterprises have found that the basic core business processes in the area of financials, logistics and human resources are not different than in the manufacturing segment. This has, to some extent, dispelled the myth that ERP solutions can be implemented only in the manufacturing or processing industries.

With the liberalization of Indian economy and the consequent competition, enterprises in India have realized the need to adopt ERP solutions. Though infrastructural bottlenecks like telecom and power exist, a number of enterprises have found innovative methods to overcome these problems and implement ERP successfully. The fact that technological advancements in India have kept pace with innovations elsewhere in the world has helped the advancement of ERP in India. Customers in fields such as automobiles, FMCG, steel and pharmaceuticals have already found that integrated systems have provided tangible benefits to their organizations.

Let us now examine examples of manufacturing industries which have reaped benefits from production-oriented information systems like ERP. A few cases of ERP implementation both in India and abroad are enumerated here to bring out actions which make ERP effective.

A top manager of a major electronic equipment manufacturing company in India used to say 'We have bought a computer to streamline our production operations.' The emphasis here is on 'We have bought', and not on the selling skills of the computer manufacturers. Also, the emphasis is on streamlining the production operations. Apart from stressing the use and the implementation of production applications, the actions taken included scientific numbering of parts, materials and assemblies; educating, the production department personnel, inculcating in them a sense of participation and insisting on only computer-based information, always. These were some of the actions that made the system effective.

The chief executive of a premier machine tool manufacturing company set the target of implementing load scheduling to the machine shop to improve the availability of beds at the required rate for manufacture of machines, time of lathes and grinders, etc. When the computer-generated schedule was implemented, it came to light that the problem was not in the machine shop, but that smaller castings were not coming out of the captive foundry at the desired rate. Weight or tonnage being the measure of output of the foundry and the number of assembled beds for lathes, etc., and not the weight being the measure of the efficiency of machine shop was the root of the problem. Soon afterwards, quantitative as well as critical part targets were set in the foundry. Also **bills of materials (BOM)** of end products were integrated with BOM for the foundry castings. These follow-up measures and periodic reviews resulting in making the ERP system effective in this particular situation.

Similarly, the effect of ERP implementation can be quantified as percentage reduction in inventories or percentage reduction in rejections or reduction in certain number of days in the production cycle. These have to be periodically reviewed and remedial measures have to be put in place in the entire production process and the system.

The problem at a factory manufacturing air-conditioning plants abroad, was that at installation time the erection engineers were finding wrong parts and unmatched parts in them. This was leading to delays in erection of the air conditioning plants and customer dissatisfaction. To overcome this problem, a specific software module called **Configurator** was developed, which was loaded on to the portable computers that the marketing people were carrying with them. With this module in an interactive session, the marketing person captured vital information used in the selection of the bill of material (BOM). The modifications of the BOM were then available electronically to the ERP software that the company had installed. Thus, the company was able to reduce customer complaints and delays in commissioning of air-conditioning plants. This illustrates that a company that implements ERP has to go beyond the conventional inputs to reap its full value.

A cable assembly manufacturing company, which has multiple plants, located geographically apart, implemented ERP to improve the demand/supply imbalance between different plants. On review of the effect of ERP implementation, it came to light that in some cases where the production rate was linked to incentive earning of workers; the effect was not of the desired level. The management then implemented a customized human resource module linked to the ERP system. Thus, the gaps in the solution were plugged and ERP became more effective. In this example, management had seen a component of salary earning as a vital link in the production process and integrated the ERP with the process and made ERP effective.

To summarize, the mere purchase of the ERP system will not yield the desired results. Top management should involve itself in all the stages of implementation of ERP, review the results and take appropriate follow-up actions. Then only ERP will be effective in any organization.

It is one of the greatest integrations of the 20th century: companies all over the world are redesigning and reengineering their business processes to reflect the changes their markets are undergoing. This is due to such factors as global competition, shorter time to market, shrinking product life cycles and rapid advancements in technology. Organizations realize that they must begin integrating processes across disparate divisions and departments. That requires a new generation of information technology (IT) solutions that bring an entire company or organization together and address a broad range of needs. Solutions that let your organization work more efficiently, respond to customers more quickly and bring products to market more rapidly.

You can get all this by implementing technology based on ERP, the new business-computing paradigm. Ideal for a range of manufacturing, processes, distribution, financial and retail business, ERP relies on a number of integrated applications,. These are used to identify the enterprise-wide resources required to service customers. ERP covers just about every area of the business.

EVOLUTION

The evolution of ERP solutions has a long history. Earlier packages used to come in different forms and in a non-integrated fashion. But slowly the need was felt to integrate various segments of an enterprise and go beyond back office and front office. With the growth of business-to-business requirements and large databases, and the rise of concepts like supply chain management, just-in-time and to-order manufacture, ERP has become a compulsory addition. In short, new dynamics of business have forced the corporates to employ ERP solutions. Shrinking geographical borders, integration of currencies, ever decreasing product life cycles, reduced profit margins and the need to raise productivity, each of these problems is addressed by ERP solutions. The physical, inventory, financial, market and human resources are to be properly pooled and maintained and ERP solution do just that.

Earlier, only global organizations, multinational companies (MNCs) and large corporations with multi-country operations considered that ERP solutions were necessary for them. But even a small company, if it is looking at the global market, has to implement ERP solutions. And now, with liberalization and international market integration, any company can target the global market and expand beyond its national frontiers.

The cost of implementation of ERP used to be high, but it is gradually coming down and now even medium and small companies can go for it. In fact, some providers are developing cheaper ERP solutions aimed at smaller companies. Some of them have also brought out ready-made templates to be used by smaller corporations.

The experience in other countries shows that the productivity levels have gone up three-fold with the implementation of ERP solutions. However, in India, we are still in the early stages of implementation and do not have information on the rise in productivity. But it will certainly help in the Indian context as well when the results start coming in shortly.

Beyond Automation

Automation was the magic word in the beginning. The focus then shifted to computers and the trend was, to run an efficient organization, throw in hardware and replace human-power with microprocessor power, pink slip the employee and hopefully the costs and the faults will come down. Not that there was much that was wrong with that approach. From then to the mid-eighties, automation was considered the panacea for all ills of business. Then the bottom simply fell out. Far too much information technology was loaded onto inefficient processes and throwing it at a mess doubly compounded the confusion.

There was an urgent need to reconfigure the existing processes and reinvent the organization, as it were. The basis of automation was that manual processes needed to be made more efficient. **Manufacturing resources planning (MRP II)** was the ultimate application for enterprise-wide automation, wherein the entire organization, starting from the sales process to the shop floor, was sought to be put online. MRP II assumes a static nature of the enterprise and fits the systems to it. As a result, MRP II automates the existing processes based on the existing workflow in the enterprise. The real benefit of MRP II is that it also enables a high degree of integration with other automated processes in the organization. To that extent, MRP II is heavily dependent upon the available hardware and software platforms in the company. Thus, if a company is already standardized on Unix it would be logical to implement an MRP II solution under Unix environment only because MRP II will integrate the other applications and will run on top of the existing platform. The second problem with MRP II is that it is an automation solution and in many cases, may not turn out to be a business solution.

Enterprise Resource Planning, on the other hand, is a business solution. The fundamental difference is that ERP will run (in most cases) in tandem with a fresh look at the existing business processes in an organization and in that sense, ERP runs in close association with **business process reengineering (BPR)** of the company. BPR will initially question the value-added potential of the particular process and then go on to put some systems and procedures in place. ERP, hence, functions as the key enabler in any BPR. But it is more applicable in those organizations which have highly developed information systems and a high degree of value-adding at every stage of the process. The key factor is that every company that implements ERP has to reengineer its processes in one form or the other. ERP is essentially an activity that encompasses the entire organization, irrespective of its size, number of plants and locations. Another significance of ERP is that it does not blindly automate and so if a certain function is not automated it may not exist. ERP takes into account not only the company internal issues, but also factors in the external imperatives in terms of competition time-to-market and soon, as a result ERP transcends the classical automation models and is considered to be the next generation of post-automation solutions.

ERP REVISITED

The business environment has changed more in the last five years than in the previous five decades. The pace of change continues to accelerate and corporations around the world seek to revitalize, reinvent and resize in an effort to position themselves for success in the 21st century. The ability to respond to new customer needs and seize market opportunities as they arise is crucial. Successful companies today recognize that a high level of interaction and coordination along the supply chain will be a key ingredient to their continued success. Enterprises are continuously striving to improve themselves in the area of quality, time to market, customer satisfaction, performance and profitability. Tomorrow's winners will be those businesses that can most effectively gather vital information and quickly act upon it. Making informed business decisions in this manner would enable organizations to accomplish their business growth while also enabling them to utilize information for competitive advantage.

To enable the companies to execute this vision there is a need for a infrastructure that will provide information across all functions and locations within the organization. The enterprise resource planning software provides this infrastructure.

Traditional Approach

Traditionally companies developed computer applications for each of the functional areas like general ledger, purchasing, inventory and planning.

Systems have always been developed as islands of information where the focus was on functions. Data was redundant and/or inconsistent and consolidation was not possible. The decision-makers of the organization did not have access to information that could help them take timely decisions and hence managerial control was difficult. Any change in the business had to be taken care of by modifying the systems that took enormous time and effort. Thus, reaction to change in the constantly changing business environment was difficult. A need was felt for an integrated system that could address these requirements. Companies started investing in an integrated system to derive competitive advantage in the marketplace.

While the MRP and MRP II packages addressed primarily the requirements of a manufacturing setup, ERP addressed the information requirements of the entire enterprise. The focus of ERP has not only been on addressing the current requirements of an organization but also on providing the opportunity for continually improving and refining business processes. Since the system was totally integrated, elimination of redundant and inconsistent data followed.

ERP AND THE MODERN ENTERPRISE

There is a saying in China: He who looks to the stars should not forget the heat of the sun. Using IT does not mean setting up computers to manage jobs. It also does not mean getting streamlined. Creating transparent departments and improving workflow IT deployment is all this and much more. If one were to choose a single word to define the importance and relevance of IT to organizations, it is **oneness.** ERP is a definition for this great commonalty that IT intends to transform most business processes into.

The Modern Enterprise Paradigm

Enterprise resource planning is a development of an enterprise-wide management system, which was also termed as MRP I, the modern version of the manufacturing resource planning system. What both these models purport to do is to integrate all the processes of the organization with the customer satisfaction side of the marketing equation. Simply put, ERP is the planning of the four Ms of an enterprise's resources, Man, Money, Materials, Machines to their best synergistic values. While earlier on, the manufacturing activities of the organization had the most to gain by implementing these tenets of MRP I, today, the whole gamut has expanded to include non-manufacturing type of industries also. So, now we have aerospace, software and hardware organizations, manufacturing, and pharmaceuticals, all trying hard to hook up to customer-oriented domains.

Businesses are realizing that customers focus means better products and services delivered fast—so fast that the customer and the market get what they need. So, for the businesses that are in the process of getting all this done there is lot happening all around. And that is the call of ERP which basically helps an organization address needs like reduced cycle time, customer focus, and sharing information seamlessly across the enterprise globally.

Where ERP Comes In

ERP is a result of the modern organizations' attitude towards how their information systems are to be configured to the new business focuses. Merely automating systems is no longer the cure. The major bottleneck in getting to build software and systems solutions for emerging BPR needs is integration. Disparate elements of an organization have to be linked together so that whenever a change in an external 'pull' takes place, the enterprise is able to adjust to it immediately and effectively. This proactive adaptability of an enterprise around redefined business objectives is called **EWI** or **enterprise-wide integration.** The trend today is that many orga-nizations are changing from function-oriented businesses to process-driven entities. ERP systems enable this not only at the information systems level but also at the applications level.

The areas of ERP deal with manufacturing as well as with finance. For an ERP solution, human resources is as germane to the whole scheme of things as distribution. In fact, the various vendors who provide ERP solutions do so in the modular manner. And this is the beauty of the whole system. ERP packages are mostly built on the **objective-oriented programming (OOP)** approach. Odyssey, and ERP software systems, are examples of this approach. This is a major advantage to users and developers alike because the real world then becomes a mirror function of the IS solution.

Today, the question that comes to mind is adaptability. Protean, a package from the US-Based Marcam Corporation provided a solution to a nationwide chain of bakery stores in no time at all by putting this adaptability feature to work. The company was able to effect a specific customer requirement of change in bag size from 3 lb to 2 lb in minutes as compared to the hours it would have taken earlier. This was done right down to the production level with the help of a single click of the mouse. By changing a single characteristic-bag size of the product in the manufacturing module of the package, the entire process got updated accordingly.

ERP also helps in getting the most out of databases and ensuring that an open system approach actually works, especially where JIT (Just In Time) is in operation. One of the premises of JIT is minimal inventory.

This does not mean that there is no virtual inventory to be taken care of. Sometimes, companies are faced with the problem or reconciling, adapting and updating such processes also. Orbit, a fabric maker in California had this problem. It was making custom chips for clients and not keeping any major inventory for this purpose. All it had was an ever-growing virtual inventory and customer database which was not being handled adequately by the existing systems. This company implemented Ramco Marshal which was able to integrate very effectively, all the processes.

PROBLEMS

1.1 What do you understand by *integrated functionality in enterprise and cross enterprise functionality*? How is each one of them achieved?

1.2 What are the various resources an ERP has to optimize? How does intelligent resource planning help this?

1.3 Why is Integrated Data Model considered the heart of an ERP system? Explain.

1.4 Discuss a case study to highlight benefits resulting from an ERP implementation.

1.5 ERP solutions have flawlessly displayed the integration of various business processes and eliminated the duplication of work across various functions. Explain this statement with a brief business life cycle of a sample company.

2

Business Engineering and ERP

An Overview

In the early nineties, 'downsize' became the battle-cry for consultants and managers in the corporate world. As the urge to consolidate new organizations flourished, business engineering came to replace the outdated and overly-simplistic views implied by downsizing. While many pro-downsizing commentators spoke of obliterating existing organizations, consultants provided insights on how to restructure a leaner, more efficient company. Such insights then paved the way for a new company infrastructure based on a combination of process-oriented business solutions and information technology. This new company infrastructure was designed to meet the challenge of creating a business environment that would optimize performance and remain flexible enough to accommodate change.

Now, throughout the world, the latest business buzzword, Business Engineering (BE) is fully underway. Various companies have created special groups, often led by senior executives, that focus solely on BE.

This chapter throws light on the significance of Business Engineering, the principles and the link between Business Engineering and Information Technology specifically ERP.

WHAT IS BUSINESS ENGINEERING (BE)?

Business Engineering revolves around information technology and continuous change. It is the constant refinement of an organization's changing needs. (Esso, Austria)

Business Engineering is the re-thinking of business processes to improve the speed, quality, and output of materials or services. (Philip Morris—European Union Region, Switzerland)

The sudden popularity of the term **business process reengineering (BPR)** has led many to dismiss it as the latest business buzzword. BPR, however, is not a passing fancy. According to Michael Hammer and James Champy, authors of the hugely successful **Reengineering the Corporation** (Harper Business, 1994), business reengineering represents the radical transition that companies must make to keep pace with today's ever-changing global markets. "In the post-industrial age we are now entering", write Hammer and Champy, "corporations will be founded and built around the idea of reunifying tasks into coherent business processes."

SIGNIFICANCE OF BUSINESS ENGINEERING

In the early nineties, 'downsize' became the battle-cry for consultants and managers in corporate America. As the urge to consolidate new organizations flourished, business engineering came to replace the outdated and overly simplistic views implied by downsizing. While many pro-downsizing commentators spoke of obliterating existing organizations, consultants provided guidelines on how to restructure leaner, more efficient companies. Such insights then paved the way for a new company infrastructure based on a combination of process-oriented business solutions and information technology. This new company infrastructure was designed to meet the challenge of creating a business environment that would optimize performance and remain flexible enough to accommodate change.

Now, business engineering has gained acceptance throughout the world. Many companies have created special groups, often led by senior executives, that focus solely on BE. The reason why so many companies are engaged in extensive reengineering efforts is that society is shifting from an age where labour and machinery drove productivity to an age where productivity depends on knowledge and information. In short, we now live in the age of information. This shift has created major social, technological, and market changes, all of which have led to the increasing importance of BE.

PRINCIPLES OF BUSINESS ENGINEERING

In the past, companies benefited from economies of scale, that is, the reduction of production costs brought about by increased output, which allowed them to offer standard products and services to large, relatively stable consumer markets and to concentrate on optimizing tasks in well-defined areas. Competition and increased customer power have now undermined the importance of economies of scale. The current relationship between a company and its customers is no longer limited to just the buying and selling of a product. It encompasses the whole gamut of business activities, from customer service, consulting and pricing, to production and shipping. With more goods available to them than ever before, consumers can now be more selective. This selectivity has caused executives to reexamine their business processes. They have discovered that organizational structures, job definitions, and work flows created to manage the growth era of the 1950–1970s are now outdated and require drastic change.

Business engineering makes companies more customer-focused and responsive to changes in the market. It achieves these results by reshaping corporate structures around business processes. BE implements change not by the complete automation of a business but rather by the redefinition of company tasks in holistic or process-oriented terms.

Only companies with innovative staff, products, and services as well as short development cycles, will be able to retain their share of the market or hope to get a bigger slice of the pie. By maximizing individual and team creativity and emphasizing a process-oriented approach, BE enables a company to realize these goals.

BPR, ERP AND IT

In the vast majority of cases, information technology powers BPR. In the past, information technology was used to help companies automate existing business processes but now, technology is being used to change those processes fundamentally. Recent developments in information technology have not only made BPR possible on a radical and extensive scale, but also more effective. Today, information technology and business reengineering go hand in hand. The merger of the two concepts has resulted in the latest concept, namely, **business engineering (BE).** BE combines the innovations of information technology with BPR's focus on better business processes. The heart and soul of BE lie in radical, process-oriented business solutions, which have been greatly enhanced by the information technology of client/server computing. Most of the ERP systems are based on the **client/server solution model** and business engineering blueprint that represent an advanced integration of business process reengineering and information technology.

While the objectives of BPR have not been altered by information technology, they have gained an extra dimension in business engineering. The main thrust of BE is the efficient redesign of a company's value-added chains. By definition, value-added chains are the set of connected steps running through a business which, when quickly and efficiently completed, add value to both, the company and the customer. Formerly, information technology was little more than a streamlining tool applied to existing value-added processes. With the appearance of enterprise software systems, information technology has now become a business-modelling vehicle that can assist in the redesigning of those processes.

BUSINESS ENGINEERING WITH INFORMATION TECHNOLOGY

While business engineering is virtually unthinkable without information technology, this does not mean information technology can be used thoughtlessly or recklessly in the business engineering process. Just as there are recognizable characteristics of successful and unsuccessful engineering efforts, there are also acknowledged guidelines for deciding how, when, or whether to apply information technology.

Before deciding upon a BE project, the management, IT users, and the IT experts must get together to chart out a company's goals and identify the key processes that affect its success. Next, those processes should be reengineered to improve their effectiveness. At this point, the BE team must establish how information technology can enhance the reengineered process. Other potential benefits of information technology should be identified, such as its role in developing a business strategy to match or exceed the performance of a company's competitors. In order to get the most out of IT, this entire sequence must be continually repeated once the IT system is in place. No matter how efficient the technology, it will never help a company achieve its business goals unless the actual business processes have been scrutinized carefully. The BE team must maximize and streamline business processes and assess whether they should be changed or perhaps thrown out, before they apply technology to them.

Cost is another important consideration. Startup costs, training costs, and networking costs all vary with the size and scope of the information technology project. Hans Visser, managing director of Ernst and Young in Johannesburg, South Africa, emphasizes the importance of implementation costs. For IT to fuel business change, Visser states, IT must help "streamline business processes to have a maximum effect with minimum resources in supporting company goals."

Along with implementation costs, the long-term financial advantages of information technology are of major interest to numerous companies. Many business executives, in fact, are more concerned with using IT to increase revenues or decrease costs and are less impressed with IT benefits such as flexibility, ease of use, and improved communication.

Financial benefits in some of the following areas are possible when IT is coupled with BE:

- Increased revenues per sales call
- Decreased inventory, hardware, administrative and operating costs
- Recaptured market share
- Reduced or eliminated overtime.

However, these financial opportunities should not be overestimated, since many of them are due more to business engineering than to information technology per se. Companies take best advantage of information technology if they already have an underlying business model and an extensive process engineering in place. Only when information technology and careful business engineering work together can companies enjoy increased revenues and decreased costs. Even so, cost saving is not always a company's main objective when applying IT to BE. A textile machine manufacturer in USA, found the combination of IT and BE helped it reach its goal of improved customer service. "We're able to take care of our customers with one phone call and one person without having to put them on hold, go through the files, research the files and return the call", explains the company vice president of finance and administration. Companies also refer to product development, sales, and marketing as areas improved by BE and IT initiatives.

Once a company has, after careful deliberation and considerable process reengineering, decided to incorporate an information technology system, the implementation of the system is usually experienced as a minor revolution. Even though the radical restructuring caused by new information technology systems upsets the status quo, it offers companies a prime opportunity to reconsider existing business processes and replace them with more efficient ones.

The effective integration of processes and their expansion into new areas become decisive factors in maintaining a company's competitiveness. The implementation of process-based software aims to achieve the full benefits of integration early on through the immediate realization of full process chains. In this way, the deployment of standard software becomes an evolving, learning experience. Companies also become focused more on permanent, goal-oriented change and less on individual success stories within the company. As in the case of Nokia Mobile Phones, Finland, successes of reengineering efforts often depend upon integration of processes. According to Markku Rajaniemi, vice president of information systems, "In the realization phase of information systems, more integration than engineering takes place". Systems not coordinated or integrated may cancel each other out and negate any gains in productivity generated by IT.

Companies might be tempted to tailor their processes individually to suit a particular market segment, customer group, or product line. Meeting this objective could, however, make an individual process uniquely and indelibly programmed into the system. If that process should ever need to be changed, companies would find themselves strait-jacketed by their own routines. Thus, the details of many diverse processes must be capable of being easily modified en-masse in response to changing market requirements. New technology, then, must never serve as a one-time vehicle in business engineering. Standard software must support the ability to adapt and change within a live environment and consider whether the underlying architecture of a new software system will support an organization's ongoing change. It is far easier for a company to adopt technology to suit the structure of the company than vice versa. Continuous responsiveness must be a central attribute of a manufactured business process. A DP manager of one of the leading organizations notes, "We see business engineering as the development of business processes according to changing requirements".

ERP AND MANAGEMENT CONCERNS

The number of companies going in for ERP systems is growing rapidly. Considering the massive investment in terms of time and money that ERP implementation involves, and the risk associated with adjusting to the changes it brings about, it is important that decision-makers have a good understanding of issues that should be the focus of their concerns. These can be divided into three categories: short-term, medium-term, and long-term. There are two short-term issues. One is compliance with problems like Y2K and a single European currency. The second is shifting from legacy systems and avoiding implementation delays. The medium-term issue for management is return on investment and the long-term issue is incorporating best practices from the industry into the company's systems and procedures.

Considerable amount of time and effort go into implementation and include a wide variety of activities like coding, testing, networking, training and people redeployment, etc. Implementation delays can result in exponential growth in costs both direct, and indirect. Hence, the question before management is, how to reduce implementation time. ERP deployment has two parts: selection and implementation. Selection involves spending time in just listening to the views of various people who are involved. Since there are bound to be differences of opinion, especially among people who are very senior in the management, it is an area which should not be left to the EDP setup alone and the senior-most managers, even the CEO, must get involved. The selection criteria should go beyond technical issues—they should include business concerns like proven expertise of the vendor, especially in the desired industry, along with support infrastructure.

Implementation time is also reduced by selecting a system that is simple and offers smart tools for system administration. A system that offers an abundance of unnecessary features can only increase the implementation time. Systems that offer a consistent interface and that support both graphical and character interfaces, also help in cutting down implementation time. As regards actual implementation time, it can be reduced by working on a proven methodology, with partners and certified consultants who are experts in their line.

In the long run, ERP must enable a company to use information as a means to gain increased competitive advantage by achieving the most effective practice in the industry. Survey results show that companies using ERP effectively are not only ahead of the competition, but are also moving ahead faster, thereby widening the gap between themselves and their competitors. Incorporating best practices also results in the company adjusting faster to changes in the environment, like competition, government policies, consumer taste and so on. Ultimately best practices translate into corporate longevity; outwardly healthy corporations have collapsed like a house of cards because of weak internals.

To conclude, decision-makers need to understand that their concerns should go beyond quick and hassle-free implementation. They must be concerned about ROI and adoption of best practices, and indeed, these must be included in their planning for ERP. Fortunately, ERP meshes very well with many management concerns like business process reengineering, total quality management, mass customization, service orientation, virtual corporation, etc., and companies taking up ERP programs, can benefit greatly.

The basic objective of implementing an ERP program is to put in place the applications and infrastructure architecture that effectively and sufficiently support the organization's business plan and the business processes. Where an organization does not have an optimized business process, the project objectives should also include "process reengineering" for two powerful reasons:

- To capture knowledge with people
- To enable dramatic productivity gains.

This will ensure that the organization's homework is complete and it is ready to undertake the implementation of ERP successfully.

PROBLEMS

2.1 Discuss the concept of Business Process Re-engineering (BPR). Should BPR precede or succeed an ERP Implementation?

2.2 Explain linkage between BPR, IT and ERP.

2.3 Illustrate with relevant case study as to how ERP solutions have led to Business Re-engineering and creation of better business practices.

3

Business Modelling for ERP

An Overview

The approach to ERP is to first develop a business model comprising the business processes or activities that are the essence of the business. This is not a mathematical model, but the portrayal of a business as one large system showing the interconnection and sequence of the business subsystems or processes that drive it. Based on business strategy and objectives (the long-range plan), a business model consisting of business processes is developed. These processes are managed and controlled by various individuals in various organizations. The ERP is developed to provide the required information to the organization to manage the processes that are part of the business model. The database is the source of information and drives the ERP.

This chapter explains the business processes that underlie a business management information system and how ERP fits into the business model built.

BUILDING THE BUSINESS MODEL

The approach to going for an ERP solution is linked with overall MIS planning and requires the development first of a business model comprising the core business processes or activities of the business. This is a diagrammatic representation of the business as one large system showing the interconnection and sequence of the business subsystems or processes that it comprises. The approach to accomplish this is depicted in Figure 3.1. The arrows denote that the planning to arrive at the process is accomplished from the top down while the MIS implementation is from the bottom up. Based on the long-range plans of the business, its strategy and objectives, a business model comprising its business processes is

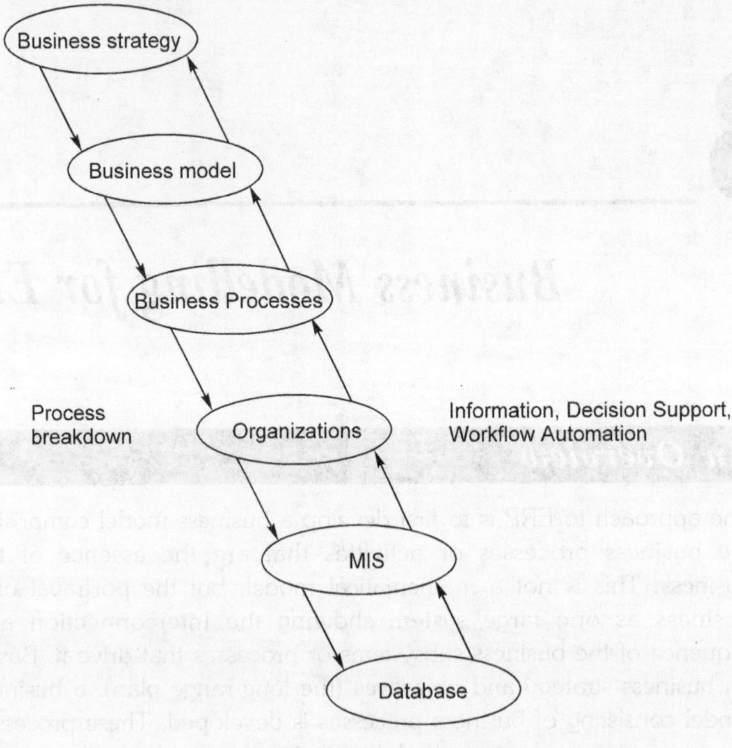

Fig. 3.1 Building an MIS.

developed. These processes are managed and controlled by various individuals in various organizations. The ERP is developed to provide the required logistic support to the organization to manage the processes that are part of the business model. The database supports and drives the ERP.

Thus, we can model a business as an integrated system making the processes managing its facilities and materials as its resources. Information, though not described as a resource, is vital in managing all other resources and can, therefore, be added as a resource while showing the concept of a business as a system as shown in Figure 3.2.

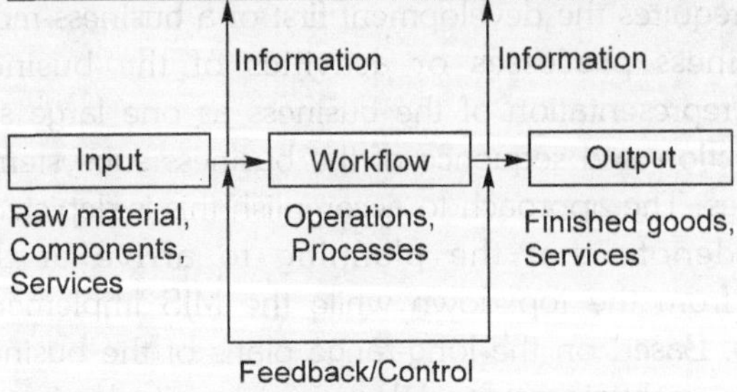

Fig. 3.2 Business as a system.

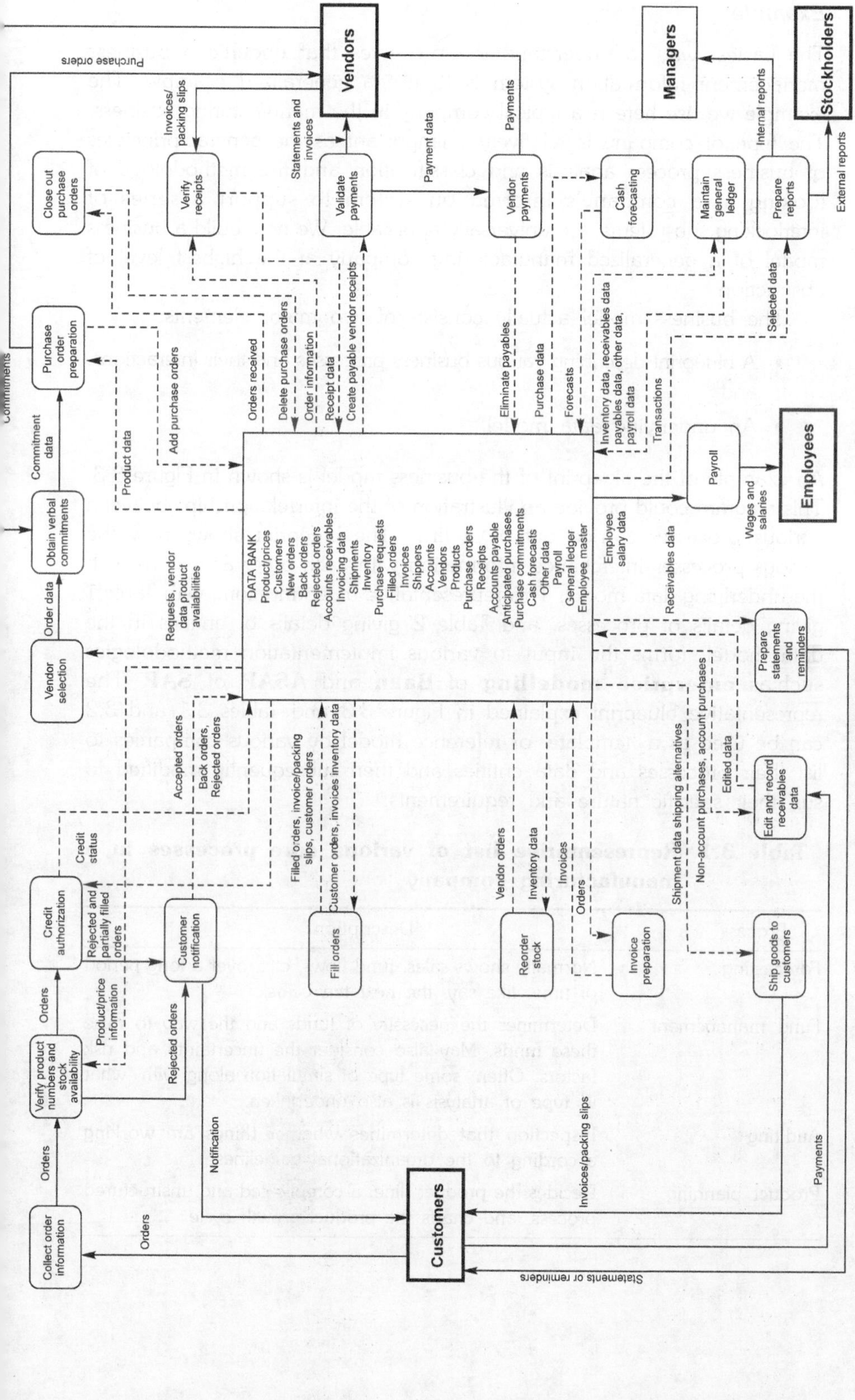

Fig. 3.3 Blueprint of a business model.

Example

The easiest way to understand the processes that underlie a business management information system is to use a generalized example. The example we use here is a typical company in the manufacturing business. The type of company is relatively unimportant as the general principles of business process analysis and classification and the methodology of looking at a company's information system to support a series of interlocking subsystems, are universally applicable. We now build a business model of a generalized manufacturing company at the highest level of abstraction.

The business model actually consists of two major elements:

- A blueprint describing various business processes and their interactions, and
- An underlying data model.

An example of the blueprint of the business model is shown in Figure 3.3. This diagram could provide an illustration of the interrelationships between various processes carried out by a firm. The blueprint shows how the various processes interchange information with each other as well as with the underlying data model. This representative blueprint along with Table 1 giving details of processes, and Table 2 giving details of entities in the data model, forms the input to various implementation methodologies such as **enterprise modelling** of **Baan** and **ASAP** of **SAP.** The representative blueprint explained in Figure 3.3 and Tables 3.1 and 3.2 can be used as a 'template' or reference model by various companies to list their processes and data entities and then subsequently modified to suit their specific nature and requirements.

Table 3.1 Representative list of various core processes in a manufacturing company

Process	Description
Forecasting	Normally shows sales, fund flows, etc., over a long period of time, like say, the next ten years.
Fund management	Determines the necessity of funds and the way to raise these funds. May also consider the uncertainty and risk factors. Often, some type of simulation along with 'what if' type of analysis is also undertaken.
Auditing	Inspection that determines whether things are working according to the organizational guidelines.
Product planning	Decides the product line, a complicated and unstructured process, and charts the product growth cycle.

Table 3.1 Representative list of various core processes in a manufacturing company *(cont.)*

Process	Description
Place planning	Concerns decisions about how the product is distributed. Also includes examining the impact of technology such as EDI. Sets procedures for determining effectiveness of the distribution channel.
Promotional planning	Consists of personnel, selling, and advertising. Includes selling a product with a sales force.
Price planning	Determines the prices at which products are offered. Involves application of technology to pricing support such as commercial database services. Also includes feedback and sensitivity analyses.
Budget allocation	Using computerized algorithms to estimate desirable mix of the funds allocated to various functions.
Product design	This process finalizes the design and technical speci-fications of the product using approaches such as CAD and CAE.
Facilities design	Includes plant layout, assembly line planning, and working out facilities to manufacture the product.
Production scheduling MRP Material requirement determination	This is the process of making new products from raw materials and generally includes production scheduling, and requirement planning. Also includes a wide variety of activities in monitoring and planning of actual production.
Quality control	This process takes care of activities that ensure that the final product is of satisfactory quality. It is concerned with identifying the existing quality gaps as well as preventing future quality problems. It involves the use of Statistical Quality Control (SQC) as well as Statistical Process Control (SPC).
Order information collection	This process deals with the collection of order information from customers by various means such as mail, phone, fax or on regular-demand and time-period bases.
Verification of orders	Includes verification of product numbers and descriptions for accuracy. Also determines whether an order can be filled or not and advises the customer regarding order acceptability.
Credit authentication	Depending upon order value, method of payment and credit status of customer, the order is approved or otherwise even though accepted as valid.
Customer notification	Informs customers about order status, integrating customers into order-processing systems, and the use of EDI, etc.
Filling orders	Involves filling of new orders, as well as back orders from available stock. Deals with various procedures regarding 'how' and 'what' of matching order quantity and stock levels. Generation of packing slips.

Table 3.1 Representative list of various core processes in a manufacturing company (*cont.*)

Process	Description
Reordering stock	Optimizes inventory-holding stocks. Decides when to order and how. It is a very crucial from the point of view of integrating suppliers into the inventory system.
Invoice preparation	Creates invoice. Also includes preparation of statement for accounts receivable.
Shipping goods to customers	Deals with activities starting from packing of goods in inventory to final loading for transportation. It should provide for a proper shipping method and suitable shipping instructions.
Editing and recording of receivable data	This process consists of editing customers' purchase transactions including packing slips, invoices, statements, etc. It also credits payments.
Preparing outstanding statements and reminders	Consists of producing information on current and past due accounts and analyzing sales patterns. Keeps track of outstanding balances.
Selecting vendors	Researches for vendors, and is mainly concerned with selection of vendors based on cost, quality and other advantages.
Obtaining order commitments	Deals with floating of requests for purchases to obtain customer quotation. The most important aspect of this process is negotiations with vendors to arrive at mutually agreed terms and conditions.
Preparing purchase orders	Includes carrying out of all necessary documentation for purchases. Increasing trend to use document management and image processing systems and EDI.
Receiving shipments	Main activities in this process are to receive and to accept or reject goods that vendors ship.
Validate payments	Deals with validating invoices and statements against actual receipt of goods and agreed terms and conditions.
Payments to vendor	Includes preparation of payment schedules based on cash forecasting. Optimization of this function may have a dramatic affect on the company.
Cash forecasting	Posting of transactions from various other processes. Ensures proper recording of revenues and expenses.
Payroll	This process produces paychecks. Should also produce data for tax purposes and keep track of various deductions such as loans, insurance, etc.

Table 3.2 Representative list of entities forming data model in a manufacturing company

Entity	Description
External data	Consists of all important entities outside the firm that interact with it such as consumers, suppliers, competitors, and distributors. Also includes predictive data regarding economy and future events occurring in external environment, labour and RM availability scenario.
Internal data	Data generated from the firm's transaction processing system, internal forecasts or parameters monitored.
Transaction processing data	This data includes day-to-day operations as well as those involving revenues and expenses. Also, sales data that result from specific mix of products.
Internal forecast data	Normally includes planning data such as expected expenses from each of the functional areas as well as sales and revenue projections from the marketing department.
Funding data	Includes information on specific sources of funds as well as availability, terms and conditions, financial obligations, and so on.
Portfolio data	Includes the current portfolio of securities held by the firm as well as their prices in the financial market.
Government regulations	Mostly government regulations pertaining to what business firms can and what they cannot do.
Strategic plan	Includes objectives, goals, mission statement, action plans. Types of product that the firm plans to supply in the market place.
Marketing research data	Mainly consumer related data that can be used to support marketing decisions, e.g. result of surveys.
Marketing intelligence data	Includes information about strategies of competitors. It is mostly semi-structured data collected through the media and commercial database services.
Production data	Shop floor data on production processes including standards and actuals of time and material resources concerned.
Inventory data	Includes inventories of raw materials, goods-in-process and finished goods.
Vendor data	Includes sources, prices, and lead times, ratings for raw material and services. It also includes products offered by vendors and their prices.
Personnel data	Mostly includes profiles of employees, their skill levels, experience and past performance on various assignments.

Table 3.2 Representative list of entities forming data model in a manufacturing company *(cont.)*

Entity	Description
Union data	Data on regulated pay scales, hiring, firing and warning conditions.
Labour data	Data about labour market, sources and prices for various skills and their availability.
Engineering specification	Includes how products can be built on standards, components and manufacturing process, drawings and libraries of specifications.
Internal marketing data	Includes internal forecasts department-wise, work centre-wise for production purposes and marketing specified standards on products.
Sales forecast	Product-wise, period-wise forecast for various products sold by the company.
Production capacity	Data about installed and available capacities of various means of production.
Production schedule	Time-based plan giving details of how products or services are going to be made available.
Inventories	Availability of all possible resources, e.g. materials in manufacturing, or seats in an airline. Does not necessarily include physical resources.
Warehouse capacity data	Data about storage capacity and distribution channels where goods or services can be stored. May be notional as in case of airline seats.
Inventory	Data about availability of RM, WIP and finished goods along with reorder level and reorder quantity and also on anticipated availability and commitments.
Shippers data	Data about agencies involved in transportation and clearing of goods along with their service capabilities and reach.
Purchase commitments	Data about specifications and features of various products or services marketed by the company.
Payroll data	Data about salaries, tax deductions, statutory forms and other deductions.
General ledger	Integrated transaction data from payroll and account receivable. Account payable. It is the basis for budgeting and planning data.

Note: Transaction data also includes entities in the form of transaction documents that store transaction data as per the respective formats. They are:

- Bill of materials
- Vendor receipts
- Warehouse capacity data
- New orders

- Back orders
- Rejected orders
- Invoices
- Accounts receivable
- Shipments
- Purchase requests
- Filled orders
- Invoices
- Accounts
- Purchase orders
- Receipts
- Accounts payable
- Cash forecast

Extended ERP

Extended ERP is a set of enterprise modelling tools for effective implementation. This is a concept promoted by The Baan Company for rapid, flexible and quality implementing of enterprise-wide software facilitating continuous improvement. These implementation tools have been developed on the basic premise that the customer should be able to implement the ERP solution with the minimum consultancy. During an implementation, the software needs to be configured to meet the specific needs of the organization. In functional terms, this means that the users need to get only the functionality that is relevant and applicable to them. From a technical point of view, this involves setting parameters and creating employee-specific menu and authorizations. Finding the relationship between these functional and technical aspects is time-consuming and costly. This applies to extended ERP also, as its base requires detailed study of the existing business model so as to generate requirements in terms of parameters to be set and configuration to be handled.

Enterprise modelling would also enable companies to graphically depict the organizational structure, functional aspects of the business model, and sequential business processes. This model enables automatic generation of each employee's menu based on the organizational relationships defined within the system. As the business model changes over time, it automatically configures the application to keep up with the business model.

Various reference business models are being worked out which are essentially process and data models that address the unique requirements of different lines of business like automotive, electronics, industrial project and process, etc. Use of these reference models gives customers a starting point for quickly mapping the ERP application to its business model and greatly reduces implementation time and effort and enhance the quality.

Business Modelling in Practice

The major task lies in defining the business model and identifying the various processes that drive it. To these processes are added various control processes as per organization policy such as the document generation process, authorization process, authentication process and so on which form the basis for subsequent implementation. Most of the ERP packages available today facilitate flow charting these processes using standard symbols. For example, SAP uses the **event-driven process chain (EPC)** methodology. By connecting all the users, event, tasks/function, organization information, they can analyze even very complex business processes. In addition, these ERP packages also provide a standard template for each of the processes, the idea being that the difference between the template process and the actual process can be easily identified. The business model also plays a very important role in selecting an ERP package as it becomes possible to identify how the package actually fits the business model under consideration.

At the time of actual implementation, a suitable data model and a MIS report substantiate the process model. By suitable analysis of the data model, process and MIS requirements, a standard data model is provided by the ERP package. Additional fields required can be identified and can be incorporated in subsequent customization. It is thus, obvious that business modelling is the base for successful ERP package selection and implementation.

PROBLEMS

3.1 Draw a business model for an organization with which you are familiar. Identify major processes and entities and show them in figure.

3.2 Carry out a study of EPC as adopted by SAP and show how it complements the generic modelling technique.

4

ERP Implementation

An Overview

Successful implementation is the obvious goal of any organization that has chosen to go in for enterprise resource planning (ERP). ERP implementation is a special event since it involves the entire organization over a period of time. It brings together different functionality, people, procedures, and ideologies, and leads to sweeping changes throughout the organization.

Given this kind of complexity coupled with time constraints that are inherent in almost all such projects, the risks involved are considerable. But what does it take to sail smoothly through the apparent rough weather of an implementation? How does one sustain the enthusiasm of the users? How do we reap the benefits of ERP in the shortest possible time?

Any company can have the best package, knowledgeable users, substantial resources, but although these elements play a part, they are not enough to guarantee the success of ERP.

This chapter discusses the roles of consultants, vendors and users, the process of customization, the precautions, the key issues, the implementation methodology and the guidelines for ERP implementation.

Successful implementation is the obvious goal of any organization that has chosen to go in for enterprise resource planning (ERP). Any ERP implementation is a special event since it involves the entire organization over a period of time. It brings together different functionality, people procedures and ideologies, and leads to sweeping changes throughout the organization.

Given this kind of complexity coupled with time constraints that are inherent in almost all such projects, the risks involved are considerable.

But what does it take to sail smoothly through the apparent rough weather of an implementation? How does one sustain the enthusiasm of the users? How do we reap the benefits of ERP in the shortest possible time? Company can have the best package, knowledgeable users, substantial resources, but although these things all play a part, they are not enough to guarantee the success of ERP.

ROLE OF CONSULTANTS, VENDORS AND USERS

Initially, organizations were skeptical about ERP since they felt that their businesses were unique and their cultures different. As time passed and their business problems became more pressing, they started looking at ERP as the panacea for their woes. In their urgency, they were expecting miracles. Unfortunately, this doesn't happen most of the time, leaving users frustrated which in turn, leads to poor participation and costly delays. It is important to understand that an ERP package cannot fit in completely with the existing business practices of an organization.

The onus to appreciate this fact is on the users and they have to work with the implementation consultants to adapt to the package. In order to avoid setbacks in an ERP project, a consultant plays a useful role. The consultants by virtue of their industry, experience and package expertise, should pitch in and set the expectations of users at various levels keeping in mind the overall business objectives of the client. They can do so by working closely with key users, understanding their needs, analyzing the business realities and designing solutions that meet the basic objectives of the company. At this point, it is also important to understand the distinction between the roles of the consultants and the users. It is the users who will be driving the implementation, and their active involvement at all levels and across all business functions is absolutely critical.

An ERP package is expected to improve the flow of information and formalize all the business processes and workflow that exist in an organization. Many users expect their workload to decrease after an ERP implementation, but this may not always happen. The important thing to understand is that the ERP package is an enabling tool to help the users do their job better, which may call for additional efforts.

If one has to have more information in a system, it entails more work for some users, but the benefit is that this information if properly stored, can be fruitfully used by other users in making better decisions. As the flow of information throughout the organization improves, the company starts performing better, and this in turn benefits the users who have collectively improved their way of working.

CUSTOMIZATION

During the course of ERP implementation, the demand for changing the core package is a common phenomenon. The scope of change may vary from a simple 'cosmetic' change to a major 'functionality' change. The consultant has to carefully weigh the impact of such changes and convey this to the users. In some cases it may be impossible to proceed with the overall project without carrying out certain alterations.

In such cases, it may be deemed necessary to customize. However, it is important to understand that customization is not expected to be the focus area of an implementation. One should try to satisfy user requirements and overall business objectives within the existing framework of the standard package because any change in an integrated system has an adverse impact on the functioning of the other modules of the package.

Besides, during the upgradation of the system, the customization exercise has to be repeated and maintenance of consistency in changes becomes a problem. This makes it more difficult to implement the package and considerably increases the risks and throws the costs and schedules out of gear. However, it must also be emphasized that implementation without any customization is easier said than done, especially when it leaves some users dissatisfied, because they feel the ERP program has not met their requirements.

It is the responsibility of the consultant to help users appreciate the fact that it is they who are ultimately benefited by implementing the standard package. This can serve to motivate and reinforce confidence among the users, who are the driving force behind any successful implementation. The success of an information system should be measured in terms of how completely it is accepted by its users. Many positive changes come about as a result of user acceptance and this becomes visible over a period of time. However, some of the benefits are instantaneous. The consultant has to drive home this fact so that the users appreciate this reality and continue to contribute positively. Ultimately, the users are certain to get a feeling that ERP is an integrator and not an intruder and as a result of this, the entire business is catapulted to newer heights and results in enhanced performance.

PRECAUTIONS

When coordination and communication are missing, one might as well forget efficiency and successful ERP implementation. A large consumer product manufacturer recently had as many as six major performance improvement programmes, including ERP implementation, going on simultaneously. Functional heads of production, marketing, finance, operations, procurement and sales were the project leaders. Each carried a different banner such as ERP implementation, reengineering, cost reduction, ISO certification, and so on.

Working in Isolation

The efforts put forward by various teams to coordinate these activities remained absent or were forced most of the time when attempts were made to formalize communication, it became bureaucratic. In other words, all the six programmes operated in virtual isolation. Though executives from various teams were invited during the steering committee meetings, the issues of governance and decision-making were fuzzy at best.

Missing the Profitability Bus

The result, as one may imagine, was that a great opportunity for improving the profitability of the organization was lost. Surprisingly, individual teams declared that their projects were a huge success and tremendous savings had accrued!

In several situations, approaches to people, processes and technologies conflicted with each other. The lack of coordination increased the redundancy of work and de-motivated the project team members. A higher-than-normal attrition rate was observed subsequently.

Not a single ERP implementation in India has reached the stability or maturity to deliver business benefits in significant measure. What went wrong?

No other management mantra in the last one year has made as much impact on corporate information systems (IS) as ERP. It has emerged as a beacon of hope that promises to solve all information-related hassles. ERP strives to create a seamlessly integrated organization that is transparent and efficient, paving the way for quick and quality decision-making. With a lot of CEOs and CIOs having decided to embrace ERP, there have been tremendous expectations and excitement regarding the benefits that such integrated systems can provide.

The Problem Statement

The basic idea of implementing an ERP solution is to get tangible business benefits that would improve the performance of the organization and achieve certain business objectives. This could be in terms of inventory reduction, faster time to market, reducing manufacturing and order processing cycle times, etc. It is amazing but true that not a single ERP implementation in India has reached the stability or maturity so far to deliver these business benefits in significant measure. Most of them still seem to be in a half-baked stage where the organizations have been unable to respond to the stringent demands and discipline required by the ERP packages. The fact that implementation of the world-class packages requires tremendous effort in enforcing change in management coupled with the inability of these firms to respond to that challenge have further compounded their problems.

Thus it has become critical to deliver value out of these implementations in a reasonably short time, so as to justify the large investment involved. This brings us to a very basic question—how do we maximize the return on IT investment? What are the factors in an ERP implementation that could maximize the Return on Investment (ROI)?

Key Issues

The three key issues that could determine the success of an ERP implementation and work towards delivering quicker and better ROI are:

1. Functionality. The ability of the package to support the best business practices followed in the company's line of business would be a crucial factor in determining the smoothness of implementation. Major gaps in required functionality can lead to time consuming and cumbersome customizations that could put time schedules and budgets off track. A focused evaluation exercise at the selection stage would help eliminate incompatible choices. The quality and commitment of business consultants and product consultants involved in the ERP implementation would also be a very crucial factor in ensuring its success.

2. Technology. Scalable ERP solutions that support open, non-proprietary technology standards would provide for protection of investment and ensure minimal risk. They should support different kinds of operating systems, databases and operate on most major client/server hardware platforms, **local area networks (LAN)** and user interfaces (ASCII Motif, Windows 95, etc.) so as to minimize risk towards technology obsolescence. The ERP package's programming language, software development tools should permit ready adaptation of the system in response to ongoing changes in production and operational processes. To minimize customization effort and time, the development tool-set for the applications should be easy to use.

3. Implementability of the solution. This would be the most crucial and significant factor as customer satisfaction and the benefit of ERP would depend not only on functionality but also on ease of configuration, ease of use and the software's flexibility to support optimization of business processes.

Much of the complexity of a software implementation process has also to do with setting of parameters, designing menus and authorizations. The roles and responsibilities of different employees have to be clearly identified, understood and configured in the system. The involvement and willingness of the employees to accept and use these new procedures laid by the ERP would, to a great extent, determine the success of the implementation. Simple, easy to use processes and procedures go a long way in creating user trust and confidence. There have been instances of large and complex packages failing to deliver on implementation because of the misgivings users had in terms of difficulty of configuration and usage.

When organizational changes take place, the software solution should grow and adapt to the changing demands of information needs. The ability of the ERP package to manage and support dynamically changing business processes is a critical and vital requirement for the organization.

ERP: POST-IMPLEMENTATION OPTIONS

After an ERP implementation, organizations should not sit back and relax. Depending on the scope of the ERP implementation exercise, several options can be explored to further maximize the gains.

The first thing that an organization should look forward to, after an ERP implementation, is improved morale of the workforce. Needless to say, it would have a cascade effect in terms of increased productivity and better customer response.

On the monetary side, depending on the level of success, ROI should also be on the way up. It is estimated that a well managed ERP project can have up to 200 per cent return on investment within a short period of time while a poorly managed ERP project can yield a return on investment as low as 25 per cent.

During the phase of minimization, organizations move closer to best practices. Depending on the **target environment design,** which is governed by the ability to change, this effort could be a natural extension of the ERP implementation or it could be a separate project in itself. Process optimization, and thus performance improvement, are a continuous exercise.

ERP IMPLEMENTATION METHODOLOGY

Broadly, the steps involved in a total ERP implementation can be listed as follows:

1. Identification of the needs for implementing an ERP package.
2. Evaluating the "as-is" situation of your business.
3. Deciding upon the desired would-be situation for your business.

4. Reengineering of the business processes to achieve the desired results.
5. Evaluation of the various ERP packages.
6. Finalizing of the ERP package.
7. Installing the requisite hardware and networks.
8. Finalizing the implementation consultants.
9. Implementation of the ERP package.

We now briefly discuss these steps:

1. Identification of the needs for implementing an ERP package. The first step for implementing an ERP package is to identify the reasons for going in for an ERP solution for your business. This step prepares you for some basic questions like:

Why should I implement an ERP package?

Will it significantly improve my profitability?

Will it lead to reduced delivery times for my products?

Will it enhance my customers' satisfaction level in terms of cost, delivery time, service and quality?

Will it help reduce the costs of my products?

Will it enable me to achieve the same business volume with reduced manpower?

Will it enable me to reengineer my business processes?

The above questions, although very obvious, should form the basis of the decision to adopt an ERP implementation and should at all times be the final goal. The other factors that should be taken into consideration are:

- Need for quick flow of information between business partners
- Effective management information system for quick decision-making
- Elimination of manual preparation of various statutory statements
- Need for a high level of integration between the various business functions.

2. Evaluating the "as-is" situation of your business. In this step, one needs to thoroughly understand what existing business processes the organization is following to transact its business. The various business functions should first be enumerated. For example, procurement, production, sales, etc. Now the processes used to achieve the business transactions should be listed in detail. The technique of process mapping can be used here. The process map should give you the following details for any business process:

- The total time the business process takes to complete
- The total number of decision points involved
- The number of departments/geographical locations that the business process involves
- The flow of information
- The number of reporting points.

3. Deciding upon the desired would-be situation for your business. In this step, we decide on what we want our business processes to finally look like. Here we use the techniques of **benchmarking** to ensure that the targets set are comparable to the best in the industry. Benchmarking can be done on various aspects of the business like cost, quality, lead time, service, etc.

4. Re-engineering of the business processes to achieve the desired results. To achieve the new business processes we reengineer the existing processes in such a manner that

- The business process cycle time is reduced significantly
- The number of decision points are reduced to the bare minimum
- The flow of information is streamlined, i.e. there is no unnecessary to-and-fro flow of information between departments.

5. Evaluation of the various ERP packages. In this step various ERP packages available in the market are evaluated with respect to the following aspects:

Global presence. Check the performance and acceptability of the package globally.

Local presence. Check how the package is performing in the local market—this gives an idea as to how well a package is taking care of the country specific business needs.

Investment in R & D. Evaluate the package from the point of view of investments the ERP vendor is making in R & D to continuously upgrade their product. A good investment in R & D is a healthy indication of the longevity of the package.

Target market. See which segment of the industry the package is basically aiming at. Some packages, for example, are specific to process industry type of applications whereas others cater specifically to discrete manufacturing. Choose a package that has a strong hold in your type of industry.

Price. This is of course the main criterion that decides what package you will finally go in for.

Modularity. This aspect needs to be considered when you want to implement only some particular functions in the ERP package. The availability of the package as independent modules is a must in this case.

Obsolescence. While considering a package it is essential to see what would be the active life of the product before it becomes obsolete. As mentioned above the investments in R & D directly contribute to upgrade a package from time to time thus increasing its useful life.

Ease of implementation. This factor needs to looked into in detail because a quick, smooth and hassle-free implementation is the key to successful transition from the legacy system. This in turn ensures that your business is not adversely affected in the transition period.

Cost of implementation. With large-scale integration of ERP packages and the consequent complexity built into them, it has become essential to consider the cost of implementation which in some cases can be phenomenal.

Post-implementation support. Before deciding on an ERP package, it is advisable to check the quality and range of the post-implementation support that the vendor provides for his package.

6. Finalizing of the ERP package. After a thorough evaluation of all the ERP packages vis-à-vis the key factors of your business, the package best suited to your business needs is selected. The process of finalizing can be simplified by making a matrix of the key factors. You can then rate all the packages under these heads.

7. Installing the requisite hardware and networks. In this step one has to install the hardware and networks required for the chosen ERP package. The installation of the hardware has to be well planned because generally the hardware arrives in time and lies idle due to the delays in implementation. Also, the induction of the hardware should be in a phased manner to avoid blocking of capital.

8. Finalizing the implementation consultants. The factors which go into the selection of the consultant are:

- Skill-set available with the consultant (application area)
- Installation base of the consultant
- Industry-specific experience (knowledge of the various industry-specific business processes)
- Finances involved in hiring the particular consultant.

9. Implementation of the ERP package. The broad steps involved in the implementation of the ERP package are:

(i) Formation of implementation team
(ii) Preparation of implementation plan
(iii) Mapping of business processes on to the package
(iv) Gap analysis
(v) Customization
(vi) Development of user-specific reports and transactions
(vii) Uploading of data from existing systems
(viii) Test runs
(ix) User training
(x) Parallel run
(xi) Concurrence from user on satisfactory working of the system
(xii) Migration to the new system
(xiii) User documentation
(xiv) Post-implementation support
(xv) System monitoring and fine tuning.

Formation of implementation team. It is of the greatest importance to form an implementation team consisting of knowledgeable users from all functions along with IT personnel and personnel from the implementation consultant. From the people chosen, the project manager, project leaders and the module leaders should be identified and also a steering committee should be formed. The functions of the steering committee are:

- To monitor the progress of the implementation
- To see to it that the schedule of the implementation is adhered to
- Resolve any problems that come up in the due course of the implementation
- Allocation of resources for implementation.

Preparation of implementation plan. An important task is the preparation of a detailed implementation plan that covers the total implementation process. Here various project management techniques like PERT charts can be used. The implementation plan should have clear components and should include the schedule for the following:

- Training of the project team
- Mapping of business processes onto the software
- Function-wise implementation
- Customization
- Uploading of data
- Test runs
- Parallel run
- Crossover.

Mapping of business processes on to the package. This is a crucial step where the reengineered business processes are mapped on to the software. In mapping, the implementation team tries to fulfil the user requirements by making use of the standard functionality available in the software. However, if the requirements cannot be covered fully by the standard system, then the next step of implementation, i.e. gap analysis comes into the picture.

Gap analysis. As mentioned above, the user requirements that cannot be directly mapped on to the standard system form the basis of gap analysis. Here, all such uncovered requirements are compiled into a gap analysis report. The 'gaps' are then classified into the following three heads:

- Gaps which can be taken care of with a little programming effort
- Gaps which involve an extensive programming effort and hence require extra resources
- Gaps which cannot be taken care of in the system.

For the first category, the project team directly takes action and resolves the issue. For the second and third category of gaps, however, the steering committee comes into the picture and decides on the extra resource allocation/process change.

Customization. Once the process mapping and gap analysis have been done, the actual customizing starts. In this step, first the customizing needs are chalked out and then the actual job is handed over to the respective functional teams.

Development of user-specific reports and transactions. As mentioned under gap analysis, any user requirements not covered by the standard system need to be provided by extra programming effort. In this step, the required reports and transactions are created.

Uploading of data from existing systems. With customizing in place, the system is now ready to receive the master and transaction data from the existing system. In this step, programmed transfer of data takes place from the existing system to the new system. To avoid wrong tabulation of master data, the transfer process needs to be thoroughly checked in the trial runs. At times it too involves a lot of programming effort.

Test runs. In this step, the test runs on the system are started. Sample transactions are tried to see whether the customizing and master data uploading has been error-free. The result of the sample transactions is evaluated and any changes required in settings to get the desired results are incorporated.

User training. The training of users can be started alongside the test runs. Users belonging to different functionalities are trained in their respective functions. Normally user training includes:

- Logging in and logging out
- Getting to know the system
- Navigating through the various menu paths
- Trying sample transactions in respective functions.

Parallel run. With the successful test runs and user training in place, the parallel run of the system can be now started. In parallel run, the business transactions are carried out both through the existing system as well as through the new system. The implementation team then takes care of any lacunae which come to light during the parallel run.

Concurrence from user on satisfactory working of the system. If the parallel run is satisfactory and error-free, or errors that may have come up have been resolved, the users may be asked for their final approval.

Migration to the new system. When the parallel run has been successfully tried for a reasonable length of time and when the users and the implementation team feel absolutely confident, it is time to go 'live'.

User documentation. User documentation includes the details on how to carry out the various transactions. It is different from the regular ERP package documentation in the sense that it is more specific in nature than general documentation. It only covers alternatives that are being used in the particular business so as to make it easy for the user to understand and use them.

Post-implementation support. Post-implementation support generally involves queries from the user, minor changes in the report formats, as well as small changes in layouts of various printed formats like purchase orders etc.

System monitoring and fine tuning. In this phase, the IT people monitor the system closely to see the performance aspects and fine tune the database and other administrative aspects of the system so that the user can derive the best performance from it.

GUIDELINES FOR ERP IMPLEMENTATION

Understand your corporate needs and culture. Readiness for change and the capability to implement that change will be the first step towards successfully choosing the right ERP-based business solution. The top management team along with the various departments must be prepared to accept that change, and to implement the ERP package.

There is a difference between seeing the need for change, and being willing to accept it. Time, and understanding the opportunity to change and the cost of not changing will help increase readiness. For example, the production planning people might be ready to change, but if the sales people are not prepared to give them product-wise forecasts, it will not work. Manual and non-ERP solutions could get away with patchwork and hazy data but the project will be undermined by the inconsistencies in data and will not succeed.

The greater the element of change involved, the greater will be the challenge in implementing it. Excellent project leaders prepare for change by first understanding the degree of difficulty they face. Often, management does not understand at the start of the project the need to change, and the interrelationships between the various functions.

An ERP implementation will bring about a change in the roles of different departments, requiring different skill-sets and changes in the authority and responsibility. In short, it will result in a change in the existing power structure. You must place this understanding within the context of your company's risk profile to define your project approach. Be sure not to underestimate the complexity of this change initiative. Remember, an ERP implementation is not an IT project.

Complete business process changes. The organization should first use the ERP implementation process to identify the changes in business processes and in skills and attitudes that must be made. While the company will be willing to do this, it may not have a complete understanding of the implications of the changes it is adopting. It will be useful for the organization to engage in a brief business process redesign exercise prior to the implementation. In that effort, however, it will have to keep in mind the structure of the ERP package so as not to design new requirements that are not supported by the package. This brings into focus the broader issue whether deploying enterprise-wide applications requires IT managers to identify their business processes before they decide on a package. Because software is so tightly integrated, making modifications to its core capabilities is difficult and often extremely expensive, or even unviable.

The cost and difficulty of changing the way a packaged system is configured after implementation are far greater than those of making an informed decision earlier.

Communicate across the organization. Obtaining support from executives is the key criterion for success. Successful feedback and a forum for top management is required to address their concerns and is also vital. Employees at all levels who are affected by the new system need to be informed by a rigorous communications programme. The key to success in this effort is repetition and a realistic setting of expectations. People need to be told several times about change.

Expectations must be managed. If they are set too high, people are bound to be upset, frustrated, and disappointed by the results. Set too low, employees will be surprised by the extent of change and will find it difficult to adapt. In either case, this will slow their ability to accept and fully use the system.

Provide strong leadership. It is very crucial for a successful project manager to appreciate and apply this success factor. Many executives can be supportive of a project but will fail to provide real hands-on leadership and commitment. The difference between informal support and active leadership can be the difference between success and failure. It is imperative to develop a steering team which must be capable of change management and the process of redesign and integration. This is not easy, as most successful managers are not trained as good business analysts. However, it is possible, with the right modelling tool, to make it easy for the managers to understand graphical business process maps and visualize the limitations and potential improvements. The same maps can be summarized for senior management to get a broad view and drill down to see the details of vertical (within the department), or horizontal (across departments) checks, tasks, delays, and hands-off operations.

The steering team must be prepared to undergo training to understand the process mapping and reengineering methodology. They should be fully involved in the redesign, else they will reduce it to a gross simplification and the team members will try and keep giving them a simplistic view of the real process. After all, most business processes can be broadly described as designing/development of a product/service, purchasing the inputs, value adding/manufacturing, and then selling.

Ensure an efficient and capable project manager. Managing a complex, large-scale project like an ERP implementation is best done by blending the organizational and IT skills, along with the management of change. A successful project manager integrates concerns that would otherwise fall between the cracks, and communicates with all those who may be involved. This requires sensitivity to three perspectives: information technology, business, and change management.

Integrated change means that these three aspects are viewed as a whole, wherein a change in one affects each of the others. In the past, IT change, business process change and the organizational and individual change were viewed as disparate elements. Each could, and usually did, trigger changes in the others. These changes have historically been carried out sequentially. So you could introduce an **IT inventory system,** make the store stocks accurate and then go in for an MRP meanwhile gradually changing the roles of the sales, production, materials and finance departments to start integrating the operations. With the advent of enterprise-wide integrated information systems, integrated change is not only available, but is required.

The result of integration in managing change means that projects are far more complex than ever before. Thus, the project and its leader must deal effectively with new technology, new business processes, changes in organization structure, and standards, and procedures that affect the jobs of individual employees, all at the same time. Unless the project leader is sensitive to the impact of each of these elements of the project as a whole, he is unlikely to successfully handle the conflicting requirements.

Choose a balanced team. The systems environment of today's ERP solutions is complex: RDBMSs, servers, nodes, application servers, LANs, WANs, networking, etc. The hardware/software package is increasingly seen as a utility, similar to the network. Customizing the software to fit the requirements of a particular function of the business will become the job of the analyst and user. There will no longer be a lot of documentation to specify the requirements. These will be on-line, as an integral part of the package. There is a shift in user responsibilities to include those which earlier lay with the IT department, e.g. response times, query searches and so on and so forth. The user becomes an expert in the integrated IT and manual processes. Hence, the business people in the project team must start thinking of the process as a whole.

This is why most ERP project teams primarily comprise individuals from the business departments who will be part of the ERP deployment exercise. They configure the systems, using the tables and functions available to run the business in the new way. After implementation, they take responsibility to maintain the systems, when changes are needed. So, if new products, price lists, statutory changes, etc. come, the user will modify the system through appropriate table changes.

Ideally, the project team must include members of the IT department, sales, materials, manufacturing, plant maintenance and finance. Additionally, the company may hire an outside consultant from an ERP consulting/implementation partner firm to provide knowledge in the concerned modules, and in project management. The IT team must be selected from the best in the company and should comprise those who have the ability to learn the new system, pick up the package's programming environment quickly and would be the first to be sent for ERP training.

Select a good implementation methodology. You may not follow every step in the process you choose, but it is extremely helpful to have a road map. It is advisable for the project leaders to set out clear, measurable objectives at the very outset, and review the progress at intervals, as the implementation progresses.

IT projects are essentially systems integration projects. They are complicated and require attention on issues such as the implications of even the slightest change. With the many modules of an ERP which interact with each other, a small change can create a ripple effect across the whole system. Up front, it is important to scope out the project. The scope should be arrived at after deliberation by the steering team and the process redesign team. That would form the starting point, or the charter for the project team. It should be treated seriously and once fixed, should not be changed.

Software and hardware requirements should be accomplished with the approval of the project manager, concurrence of the steering committee, and a review of the impact of the change on project schedules. The temptation to agree to change must be resisted, and a proper configuration control mechanism must be put in place.

A good practice would be to choose a good implementation methodology, preferably one where guidelines are available for determining the effort (in man months/hours) required for carrying out the various activities. It is important to scope the project, adding the step-wise and task-wise man hours required, and then working out a project plan, using project management tools. Following this there should be a walk-through with the project team, implementation consultants, and the steering committee to arrive at a realistic project plan, consciously reviewing the activities where you are deviating from the methodology, so that there are no surprises. It must be ensured that the activities dropped will not impact the quality of the system, and there must be no compromise on the resources and times required. The project leader must be bold enough to put up a fight if unrealistic schedules are demanded. Here again, the methodology will come to his rescue.

Train everyone. A new system inevitably means new ways of adapting and operating. The requirements of an ERP solution will trigger off a process reengineering exercise and the users must be informed about the needs for such a change, from the company's perspective as well as from that of an individual.

The steering team should be trained in process analysis and redesign, and given an overview of the ERP package functions and processes. The project leader should be trained in project management techniques, the users in the project team will need functional training in the package, and customization. The IT people need to know the package architecture, tables, design and configuring, the departmental and sectional managers need to know how the new system will work, and the individuals need to know the operations and the keys to press, etc. In addition, they will have to be involved in the creation of master files and records transactions for the new system, the transition process, the parallel/pilot runs, and the cut-over dates, etc.

All this will require extensive training at various levels. This training need will be greater for organizations that have not implemented on-line systems before.

Commitment to adapt and change. An ERP implementation should not be looked upon as a short distance run. It has wide implications, and will impact the future of the company for many years to come. Implementation, if it is to be effective, is a long-drawn out process. All the above factors have to be kept in mind for successful implementation. The project will not yield quick benefits and the management must be patient with the project team. An ERP project is perhaps more complex than physically putting up a new plant as it involves many changes. If you do not have the heart to change, you should not opt for an ERP solution.

However, having made up your mind to implement an ERP solution, roll up your sleeves and then march ahead. It will be a tough job, involving a lot of change and could alter the basic working of your company. Do not do it unless you consider it worth all the efforts and resources in terms of money and time, especially of the best people in your organization.

PROBLEMS

4.1 What are the steps involved in an ERP implementation? Is ERP implementation same as ERP package implementation? Give reasons for your answer.

4.2 Whose responsibility is it to carry out ERP implementation? Explain.

4.3 When can it be said that ERP implementation is over? What is to be done during Post Implementation Phase?

4.4 Explain, with the help of an example, the concept of *Customization*.

4.5 How is the strategy of selecting an ERP solution related to Business/ Corporate strategy? Elaborate using company scenario.

4.6 Enlist the general problems faced during implementation of ERP and the solutions for it.

5

ERP and the Competitive Advantage

An Overview

The essence of strategy stems from the need for companies to gain a detailed understanding of their current and future markets. Functions are then required to develop strategies focused on supporting the characteristics of agreed markets. However, functions should not be reactive within this procedure. On the contrary, they must be proactive in strategic debate, explaining their perspectives so that the rest of the business understands them. This ensures that these perspectives form part of the discussion. Manufacturing strategy, therefore, consists of the strategic tasks which manufacturing must accomplish to support the company's order-winners and qualifiers relating directly or indirectly to the function. This chapter discusses how a company should qualify in a competitive environment and win orders using ERP as the tool.

ERP AND THE COMPETITIVE STRATEGY

The essence of strategy stems from the need for companies to gain detailed understanding of their current and future markets and the factors that help them gain a competitive advantage in the field. Various organizational functions are then required to develop strategies based on the corporate practices which can give the user a competitive advantage. This ensures that these perspectives form part of the discussion. Corporate strategy, therefore, consists of the strategic tasks that the ERP vendor organizations must do to support the company's order-winners and qualifiers relating directly or indirectly to the various functions in the organization. During the 1970s, a number of organizations started using IS/IT in ways that fundamentally changed the way in which their business was conducted, and changed the balance of power in the industry with respect to competition, customers and suppliers.

It is observed that typical expressions of corporate strategy to gain competitive advantage include such general terms as service, responsiveness to and meeting of the customers' needs. In addition, there have been generic statements concerning corporate strategy formulation with expressions such as low cost, differentiation, and critical success factors. The use of generic terms similar to these breeds two major drawbacks. First, the difference is not brought into focus but is blurred, and second, decisions concerning the nature of the market segments in which a company wishes to compete are not resolved at the strategic level. A company may not recognize that orders for products, often within the same market segment, are won in different ways. This lack of clarity brings conflicting demands on the various corporate strategy functions and disperses the essential coherence necessary to provide strategic thrust, guidance and competitive advantage.

In order to gain a sustained competitive advantage, an analysis of markets at the micro-level is essential. When the chief executive officers were asked whether the markets served by the group of companies under their control were similar in nature, most of them answered in the negative. When looked at in detail and asked whether the markets served by a typical company are the same, the answer would again be 'no'. Hence, a detailed analysis of the market will throw up different qualifiers and order winners and thus necessitate a change in the erroneous belief that manufacturing and support processes in terms of processing requirements and infrastructure investments would be the same. The situation being what it is, the companies should next apply the same manufacturing approaches to support their different markets not only in one plant but in all their different plants. It means multi-mode operation support is necessary to derive a competitive advantage which is one of the essential bases for any ERP solution, as mentioned in Chapter 1.

The strategic process, therefore, needs to be based on a clear understanding of the markets and the differences within a market. As highlighted earlier, however, all too often companies debate strategy in general terms and undertake strategy using general courses of action. This invariably and increasingly leads to a lack of fit between functional strategies and corporate markets. Where this happens, companies will find themselves at a serious disadvantage. Supporting logically different markets within the same physical market with the help of the necessary infrastructure and integration at the process level is an essential feature of ERP solutions.

Thus, the absence of a strategy within a business, which identifies the qualifiers and order-winners at the highest level, typically leads to a strategic vacuum and that void, unless it is filled, will result in solutions including ERP implementation, which will not yield any significant advantage.

The foregoing discussion brings out a basic logic. Executives recognize that ERP, as a significant part of the company's infrastructure, must make, and in fact needs to be making, a significant contribution to the overall success of the business. There is, therefore, due pressure on those responsible for ERP solutions to respond to these corporate demands and expectations. Without strategic context, however, IS/IT, where ERP has been treated as a part has traditionally responded by undertaking currently popular solutions. In this way, companies seek to achieve productivity in operations by modelling operations on best practice. However, although a solution may be good in itself, its application to the specific problem is often inappropriate. (Given IS/IT's and ERP's infrastructural nature and the existence of corporate initiatives, it is easy to see why most companies have invested regularly and significantly over the years in responses that, by and large, are eventually discarded.) The cause of their abandonment is principally the lack of relevance of the ERP solution in the first place to gaining the competitive advantage in a focused manner.

Understanding the Markets

To formulate IS/IT (ERP solution) like any other functional strategies, a company must first clearly understand and agree about the markets in which it wishes to be today and in the future. This critical initial step provides the two essential dimensions for the formulation of sound and effective strategies for gaining a competitive advantage.

1. The in-depth study and discussions about the markets in which a company decides to compete is an essential prerequisite for strategy formulation. The identification and realization of competitive advantage is based on a well articulated understanding of market needs and the implications of these for all functions. It is through this mechanism that functional differences are reconciled with each other and markets and corresponding segments are delineated. Furthermore, since markets are dynamic, this strategic analysis of the markets must be an ongoing exercise.
2. With market function integration achieved, all functions should be geared toward operating in synergy in meeting the requirements of a firm's current and future markets. Thus, each function's strategic contribution is expressed in terms of its priorities, infrastructure developments and investments.

Hence, even in ERP implementation, the first step is to understand the markets. To do this adequately, companies need to set aside generic, broad-based statements, to identify the levels of difference that exist between segments, and the relevant dimensions of each segment in which they wish to compete. In order to derive any competitive advantage, there is a need to identify the differences in the markets as per the strategy formulation. To this end, an essential part of the ERP implementation task is to recognize and apply the concept of order-winners and qualifiers.

Qualifiers are those criteria that a company must meet for a customer even to consider it as a possible supplier. For example, customers increasingly require suppliers to be registered under the ISO 9000 series. Suppliers, therefore, who are so registered have only achieved the right to bid or be considered. Furthermore, they will need to retain the qualification in order to stay on the short list or be considered as competitors in a given market. However, simply providing or attaining these criteria does not win orders. Order-winners are those criteria that win the order. One of the key goals of ERP implementation is to enable an organization to realize its order-winners and qualifiers efficiently.

Order-winners vis-a-vis Qualifiers

The need to identify the micro-level market difference is further underscored by recognizing the essential difference between these two dimensions in a given market. To provide qualifiers, companies need only to be as good as their competitors; but to provide order-winners, they need to be better than them. However, qualifiers are no less important than order-winners. They are, however, different. Both are important in companies to gain a competitive advantage and thus maintain their existing market share and to even improve it.

The need to distinguish between those criteria that win orders in the marketplace and those that qualify the product to be there is highlighted in the following example. When Japanese companies entered the colour television market, they changed the predominant criteria on the basis of which products won orders from the price to the product quality (in terms of conformance) and reliability of service. The relatively low product quality and reliability of service of existing television sets meant that in the changed competitive forces of this market, existing producers were losing orders to Japanese companies because of the better quality of their product, that is existing manufacturers were not providing the criteria that qualified them to be in the marketplace. By the early 1980s manufacturers who lost orders raised the product quality so that they were again qualified to be in the market. As a result, the most important order-winning criterion in this market has reverted to price.

Corporate strategy, therefore, must provide the qualifying criteria to get into or stay in the marketplace. These alone, however, will not win orders. They merely prevent a company from losing orders to its competitors. Once the qualifying criteria have been achieved, companies then have to turn their attention to the ways in which orders are won, and they should try to execute these better than anyone else. At this level, the strategy should clearly outline the role, the ERP is going to play with respect to achieving these objectives.

Also, if price is not the predominant order-winner, it does not mean that a company can charge what it wishes. Although it needs to recognize that it does not compete on price and, therefore, should exploit this opportunity, it has to keep its exploitation within sensible bounds. Failure to do so will result in the company losing orders increasingly to those who price their product more competitively. Hence, in this situation a company will have turned a qualifying criterion (that is, a product highly priced within some limits) into an order-losing criterion where the price has become too high.

Order-winners and Qualifiers: Some General Categories

As mentioned earlier, there is a range of order-winners and qualifiers and not all of them form part of a corporate's strategic function. This section, therefore, separates the different categories and reviews typical criteria within each category. As stressed earlier, strategy is market- and time-specific and, therefore, not all order-winners and qualifiers will relate to or be of the same importance to all companies.

Here we discuss those order-winners and qualifiers that are general to most of the companies and will, wherever relevant, form the basis of the companies' strategy for getting a competitive advantage.

1. Price. In most of the markets, and particularly in the growth, maturity and saturation phases of the product life cycle, price becomes an increasingly important order-winning criterion. When this is so, the basic task of all the functions is to provide the low costs necessary to support the price sensitivity in the marketplace, thus creating the level of profit margin necessary to support the business investment involved and create opportunity for the future. This requires setting up of stringent cost targets and their rigorous monitoring besides innovative cost reduction techniques, such as value analysis. Hence, the ERP solution implementation must focus on and result in highlighting the pockets of significant cost that will give direction to the areas where resource allocation should be made and management attention given.

Where price is an order-winner, the ERP solutions must clearly come out with strategies to give the company a clear plan to reduce costs in order to maintain or improve available margins. Thus, when a company decides to use price reduction as an order-winner, it must similarly change all the related elements of its corporate strategy. Companies that elect to alter the role of price would need, therefore, to assess the lead times and investment implications, and the cost reduction potential. Making a strategic decision to reduce price without assessing these factors will invariably lead companies into inappropriate strategies, for the decision to reduce price, although difficult to evaluate, is easy to make. Cost reduction, on the other hand, is easy to evaluate but difficult to achieve unless you have a proper corporate strategy involving the specific role of ERP, as and where necessary ERP is in place.

2. Delivery reliability. *On-time delivery (OTD)* means supplying the products ordered on the agreed due date. It is normally of major concern to the entire supply chain, particularly the distribution functions. In many businesses, this criterion now constitutes a qualifier and often, it is an order-losing sensitive qualifier, meaning that if companies continue to miss due dates, customers will increasingly stop considering them as potential suppliers. Thus, unless these firms improve their OTD, they will not get the chance to compete. There is growing recognition of the importance of delivery reliability as a criterion in most markets. Its change to being a qualifier is part of that competitive perspective. Increasingly then, OTD performance is a competitive factor and its measurement by the customer, sector and overall, is a crucial consideration in most businesses. The need to identify different OTD expectations is a critical step here as with other order-winners and qualifiers and can be achieved through successful ERP implementation.

For the companies, this involves considerations of capacity, scheduling and inventory, principally for work-in-progress (WIP) and finished goods. In fact, meeting OTD involves complete management of the supply chain and synchronization of all the support groups within the supply chain. Typically, these groups, as a whole, and individually, may not synchronize with the primary functions of making and delivering products. ERP solution implementation should permit each of these disciplines to have a view of the entire supply chain so that all groups, can work towards this common aim in an integrated fashion.

The exactness of the due date can vary from an appointed hour on a given day to delivery of the agreed quantity starting, and finishing, in an agreed week. The level of data collection and the timing and proactive nature of the feedback to customers will need to form part of this decision. As a rule, the more exact the agreed delivery is, the more proactive should a supplier be in the data collection and the more regular the performance summaries and feedback to customers. Any ERP solution should be capable of processing these data as the source of information about the size of 'call-offs', i.e. what a customer actually wants rather than the total quantities expressed in any contract or agreement, and the lead times associated with the delivery. In fact, a well-selected and implemented ERP solution should be able to break the departmental deterrents to this.

3. Delivery speed. A company may win orders through its ability to deliver more quickly than its competitors, or to meet the delivery date required when only some or even none of the competitors can do so.

Products that compete in this way need an ERP solution that can respond to this requirement. There are two perspectives to the issue of delivery speed. One is where the process lead time, while being shorter than the delivery time required by the customer, is difficult to achieve because the current forward order load (or order backlog) on manufacturing capacity plus the process lead time to complete the order is longer than the delivery time required. This is resolved through either a short-term increase in capacity (such as overtime working), a rescheduling of existing jobs, or a combination of both.

The other is where the process lead time is more than the customer's delivery requirement. In these situations, manufacturing (for a given process technology) can only meet the customer's delivery requirement by either increasing short-term capacity or holding inventory and thus, reducing the process lead time by completing part of the manufacturing process before the order point in anticipation of winning these types of orders. Schedule changes may facilitate the accomplishment of the task, but will not in themselves resolve this type of situation. Where process lead time and existing order backlog do not exceed the customer's delivery requirement, delivery speed is not an issue.

With regard to delivery, it is important to distinguish between delivery promise (that is, committing the company to delivery in line with a customer's requirements) and delivery speed. The latter can be a commitment.

Increasingly, companies are reducing lead times. Some are endeavouring to shorten them reactively, if not proactively, in line with their perception of their markets or to get a competitive edge. This is increasingly becoming a key order-winner as with proper planning and strategic input where the levels of improvement that can be achieved are incredible, as shown in Table 5.1.

Table 5.1 Superfast producers

		Time from order to finished goods (Weeks)	
Company	Product	Old	New
GE	Circuit breaker boxes	3.0	0.6
Motorola	Circuit breaker boxes	3.0	0.05
Hewlett-Packard	Electronic test equipment	4.0	1.0
Brunswick	Fishing reels	3.0	1.0

Source: G. Stalk and T.M. Hout, Competing against Time: How time-based competition is reshaping global markets (New York: Free Press, 1990), p. 67 (*reproduced with permission*).

An organization's response to reducing lead times needs to be corporate-wide, and often the lead times associated with before and after manufacturing can be a substantial part of the time it takes from order entry to customer delivery. Working with the help of an IS/IT (ERP) solution, companies have been able to reduce, among other things, the lead time required to fill an order by 50 per cent. With the enormous growth in computer power, and the use of ERP solutions, there has been a tremendous reduction in prices and hence increasing pressure to reduce lead times. Staying with these developments in integrated solutions being provided by ERP solutions, the suppliers can respond to the short lead time demands of customers.

4. Quality. Quality as a competitive criterion has gained tremendous importance from the late 1970s. Although its importance has been recognized throughout, many companies have failed to compete on this dimension. In part, this is because the definition of quality has broadened to encompass many dimensions. The result has been a lack of understanding and subsequent lack of direction in terms of strategic inputs. Table 5.2 lists dimensions of quality and identifies the functions that would typically assume prime responsibility for its provisions.

Table 5.2 The dimensions of quality and the functions typically responsible for their provision

	Dimensions of quality	Functions
Performance	A product's primary operating characteristics	Design/ manufacturing
Features	Secondary characteristics, the 'bells and whistles'	Design
Reliability	The probability of a product malfunctioning within a given period	
Conformance	The degree to which a product is manufactured to the agreed specification	Manufacturing
Durability	A measure of a product's life in terms of both its technical and economic dimensions	Design
Serviceability	The ease of servicing (planned or breakdown) to include the speed	Design and after sales service
Aesthetics	How the final product looks	Design
Perceived quality	How a customer views the product	Marketing and design

While on the subject of inputs for quality assurance, the strategy should delineate the best practices and thus must be studied in comparison with existing practices in various functional processes. The role, which ERP implementation can play in closing the gap between the best and existing practices, must be an important consideration in decisions concerning selection and implementation of ERP solutions.

5. Response to demand increases. In today's markets, a company's ability to quickly respond to increases in demand is an important factor in winning orders. These sales may reflect the high seasonality of customers' requirements or be of a spasmodic or one-off nature. This factor concerns the level of predictability surrounding demand itself as well as other considerations such as product shelf life and the frequency of product modifications in line with market requirements. A quick and positive response to these variations and changes will result in a significant competitive advantage and hence forms a relevant corporate strategic dimension.

Knowing the seasonal demand makes it possible for agreement to be reached between the supplier, manufacturer, distributor and customer about inventory holdings throughout the process, process capacity, and planned increases in labour (such as working or additional shifts). With one-off or spot business (for example, during an influenza epidemic when the demand is for one product that may have a short shelf life thus limiting viable inventory levels or where a product is customer-specified at some point in the process and, therefore, cannot be made ahead of demand or a significant order for a product over and above agreed call-off quantities or simply an unexpected, sizable order for a given product), holding materials or other forms of capacity, arranging short-term increases in labour capacity (for instance, through overtime), rearranging priorities, or some combination of these will typically be a supplier's response.

The phenomena described here provide another example. A lack of essential clarity can lead to serious levels of corporate misunderstanding. The generalized discussion surrounding these key aspects of a business typically involves words such as *flexibility*. However, the extent to which a company intends to respond to these significant increases in demand is a strategic decision of some magnitude. To allow each function to respond according to its own interpretation invariably leads to major mismatches. Thus, providing this sort of flexibility in the entire supply chain management is the key aspect to be examined while considering *ERP solutions*. It should also be imperative to answer the question of 'How is the ERP implementation going to provide the instant information and integrate different activities required to make this flexibility possible in the supply chain?'

6. Product range. As highlighted earlier, markets are increasingly characterized by difference, not similarity. However, the balance between levels of customization and the volume base for repetitive manufacturing has to be addressed by bringing together the relevant parts of the organization to select from alternatives. Given that the markets are increasingly segmenting into niche areas, it is the corporation's top management's role to continue to develop processes that are flexible enough to cope with product-range differences and provide low-cost results. It needs, therefore, to be able to bridge these essential differences in order to retain the volume base so essential to efficiency while addressing niche areas.

Thus, where product ranges are widening, process developments need to reflect the broadening nature of the product base and the lower volume implications that tend to go hand in hand with these trends. The former needs to be recognized at the time when process investments are made. The latter is reflected in reduced set-up times, whether manual or automated (for example, a numerically controlled facility), so enabling companies to cope with the lower-volume nature of these changes while retaining the necessary levels of cost.

Examples of these trends are seen in the automobile industry. The pressure on car makers at the lower end of the volume scale is to continue to differentiate their products as a way of competing not only with their traditional competitors, but with makers at the higher end, of the volume scale as well. BMW's 7 series offers a marked uplift in customization, more akin to the very low-volume luxury makers such as Rolls Royce and Aston Martin. Handcrafted leather interiors and its any colour option are examples of this. However, BMW is also aware that Toyota is already planning a production system capable of responding speedily to individual customer requirements. As with all companies, to support increases in product/colour range options successfully, manufacturing needs to develop its processes to provide these in a cost- and time-efficient way. At the moment, BMW's nonstandard colour option takes extra time and cost because paint lines have to be cleaned out. A priority in manufacturing is, therefore, to develop a paint-spraying capability to reduce this problem. Looking beyond, manufacturing and assembly have to be extended to the entire organization including support functions such as purchase. In most of the cases, it is tantamount to a scenario where much backward and forward planning coupled with simulation can be carried out in rapid time to support measures taken by manufacturing and assembly line. Thus, ERP solutions by virtue of integrated functionality and shared common database, may play a major role in providing these capabilities, particularly those who have in their domain, **intelligent resource planning (IRP)**.

ERP's Role in Gaining Competitive Advantage

In the past, manufacturing companies have searched frantically to gain better control of order-winners and qualifiers. The advent of ERP has brought about an organized approach to managing order-winners and qualifiers, as they need an integrated perspective to do so. ERP has tried to handle this process by providing answers to the following questions:

1. What information do we need to manage the order-winners and qualifiers and what data model is required to support it?
2. How can groupware, workflow and document management technology be integrated to improve communication among work groups, manage paper documents by routing them electronically, and control data so as to enable organizational processes to realize relevant order-winners and qualifiers?

ERP has also helped organizations realize order-winners and qualifiers by providing a software that facilitates modelling of logistic processes in terms of items, bill of materials, routing and also registering the goods flow in the processes in terms of production order and inventory. Support for making decisions based on logistic processes is built into these packages today. The intelligent resource planning which is built into many of these packages provides advanced material and capacity planning facilities so as to take care of order-winners and qualifiers in a specific situation.

PROBLEMS

5.1 What do you understand by the term *competitive advantage*? How should an organization go about achieving it?

5.2 How can an organization use ERP implementation to obtain competitive advantage? Explain.

5.3 Survey literature or/and Internet for published literature on how ERP has helped in achieving competitive advantage. Produce a comprehensive report on it.

6 The ERP Domain

An Overview

Enterprise resource planning implementation is one of the fastest growing segments in the information technology industry today. To take advantage of emerging technologies and business practices and meet the evolving business requirements of a thriving industry, are ERP vendors who are vying for a share of this ERP market. Companies like SAP AG, Baan, Qad, IFS, Ramco Systems, to name a few of the leading ERP vendors, leave no stone unturned to capture this holy grail. This chapter highlights the key features of some of the leading ERP packages now being marketed.

Today, many organizations face continuous demands from rapidly changing and increasingly competitive global markets. They also must serve customers who want innovative, high-quality products that feature special options. Additionally, further pressures are created by technology developments that shorten many product life cycles, and by intensified international competition, which drives corporations to reduce costs and improve production efficiencies.

To increase competitive advantage, companies require flexible business information systems that adapt to rapid change. To address these needs, enterprise business applications must provide solutions that concentrate on the customer by integrating the supply chain. These systems must allow information access throughout the enterprise and provide software that adapts to the business. In addition, technical requirements include a true client/server computing environment that supports relational database technology and graphical user interfaces. Most importantly, these systems must provide open systems through choice and integrate the complete supply chain infrastructure, connecting whatever systems an organization has selected to meet its information technology requirements.

Enterprise resource planning implementation is one of the fastest growing segments in the Information Technology industry today. To take advantage of emerging technologies and business practices and meet the evolving business requirements of a thriving industry are ERP vendors who are fighting for a market share of this 'holy grail' of process management—ERP. Companies like SAP AG, Baan, Qad, IFS, Ramco Systems, SSA, to name a few of the leading ERP vendors, leave no stone unturned to capture this market.

We will take you through the key features of some of the leading ERP packages available. Please note that the information provided on the various ERP packages is compiled from the brochures and other information that is available on the net.

MFG/PRO

MFG/PRO is the flagship product of Qad, an ISO 9002 certified company, which started operations in 1979. The products currently marketed by Qad are MFG/PRO, Qwizard, Decision Support, and service/support management. The software is available in 26 languages with more than 3,600 installed sites in over 82 countries.

MFG/PRO software, provides multinational organizations with an integrated **global supply chain management** solution that includes manufacturing, distribution, financial, and service/support management applications within an open system environment. This comprehensive ERP package supports host and fully-distributed client/server applications. Component-based application development enables flexible and scalable architecture to ensure a sound path for future growth. Qad's time-to-benefit methodology makes MFG/PRO quick to implement and easy to use and maintain.

MFG/PRO's Windows-based graphical user interface (GUI) is an intuitive navigational tool that simplifies the learning process. MFG/PRO is a fully integrated software package available on a module by module basis. MFG/PRO addresses the entire manufacturing spectrum from repetitive to configure-to-order. It is appropriate for process, batch process, make-to-stock, configure-to-order and repetitive manufacturing environments.

MFG/PRO—System Modules

Distribution. The distribution modules of MFG/PRO are used to monitor inventory balances and manage purchasing and sales order entry activities. For convenience and clarity they are split into the following menus.

Inventory control. Inventory control functions are used to monitor inventory balances, perform cycle counts, review inventory transaction history, and access lot/serial tracking reports.

Physical inventory. Physical inventory functions are used to assist in carrying out annual physical inventory counts.

Purchasing. The purchasing module is used to manage material procurement, from the initial requisition and order through to the item receipts and returns.

Supplier schedules. Supplier schedules allow generation of supplier releases incorporating a set of scheduled receipt dates and quantities.

Sales quotations. The sales quotation module allows the user to maintain, trade and analyze customer quotations.

Sales orders/invoices. The sales order module provides functions to process customer sales orders and invoices.

Customer schedules. The customer schedules module provides the capability to process customer releases using a set of scheduled shipment dates and quantities rather than discrete sales orders.

Configured products. The configured products module enables the processing of orders for products which are specified at order entry time from a selection of predefined features and options.

Sales analysis. The sales analysis module provides a way to monitor salesperson productivity and effectiveness at maintaining margins, to provide visibility on sales by product line or by item, and to rank items by sales, margin or quantity.

Manufacturing. The manufacturing modules are used to regulate all manufacturing activity within the various types of production environments. They are divided into the following modules:

Product structures. The product structures module is used to define what materials and assemblies are used to manufacture a product.

Routings/Work centres. Routings/work centres is used to define the departments, work centres, operations and routings involved in the manufacture of a product.

Formula/Process. The formula/process module is used to define what ingredients and processes are used in the formulation of a product batch.

Work orders. The work orders module is used to authorize and control the manufacturing of products, record material issues and receipts, and to control rework and scrap.

Shop floor control. The shop floor control module is used to plan and report on the labour used in the manufacture of a product.

Repetitive module. The repetitive module is used to streamline labour, material planning and reporting for products manufactured in high volumes.

Quality management. The quality management module is used to define and record the quality of products. This includes inspection and testing during the manufacturing process, incoming inspection of purchased items, and inventory sampling.

Financials. The financial modules interface with the distribution, planning and manufacturing modules to report the financial implications of the company's activities.

General ledger. The general ledger module is used to record all financial transactions for the purpose of monitoring account balances and producing financial statements.

Multiple currency. The multiple currency module is used to maintain currency conversion rates and to control the calculation of currency-related transactions.

Accounts receivable. The accounts receivable module is used to track customer balances, monitor credit, produce statements and record customer payments.

Accounts payable. The accounts payable module is used to track supplier invoices, select items for payment, and generate checks or electronic funds transfers.

Payroll. The payroll module is used to generate paychecks, calculate payroll taxes, and track payments and deductions.

Cost management. Cost management is used to simulate various costs for products to aid in cost analysis and projections. It can also be used to maintain costs by site, either using a standard or average costing approach.

Cash management. The cash management module is used to plan cash requirements and to allow input of cash transactions in a "cash-book" approach.

Fixed assets. The fixed assets module provides the capability to maintain, depreciate and retire fixed assets such as buildings and plant equipment.

Service/Support. In addition to the other core modules, service/support modules are designed for companies who not only manufacture and sell their products, but also offer after-sales service and support.

Supply chain. Supply chain management is the control of goods and information from supplier to customer.

Master files. The master files function provides access to a series of foundation modules that are used by the rest of the MFG/PRO applications. These master files include: items/sites, addresses/taxes, inventory control settings, physical inventory, multiple database configurations and manager functions.

Custom. This menu item is reserved for customer-developed applications and linkages to external systems.

Solution components

•Accounts Payable •Accounts Receivable •Advanced Configurator •Advanced Pricing Manager •Capacity Requirements Planning •Cash Management •Compliance •Configured Products •Cost Management •Customer Schedules •Decision Support •DRP •EDI •Fixed Assets •Forecasting •Formula/Process •General Ledger •Management •Inventory Control •Physical Inventory •Pricing and Promotions •Product Change Control •Product Configurator •Product Line Planning •Purchasing •Quality Management •Release Management •Repetitive •Resource Planning •Routings/ Work Centres •Sales Analysis •Sales Orders/Invoices •Sales Quotations •Service/Repair Orders •Service and Support •Shop Floor Control •Validation •Warehousing.

The MFG/PRO software solution combines robust functionality with extensive technology choices, allowing you to implement your strategy for integration, computing platforms, and distributed processing.

Decision support—Features

•Real-time decision support •Power browse with multilevel drill down capability •Automatic generation of MFG/PRO-style reports •Integrated data store •Separation of data entry and reporting •Rapid configuration of new browses and reports •Rapid time-to-benefit •Definition of new key performance indicators •Extreme flexibility •Definition of new reporting categories •Browses optionally updated on-line •Multiple databases, sites, currencies •Summarization by predefined calendars.

Managers in every manufacturing enterprise rely on ERP data for tracking progress, evaluating status, and determining results. However, ERP data is traditionally a standardized set of categories reported against standardized key performance indicators (KPIs). Customization of reports, or the database itself, is slow and the result is as inflexible as the original package. Decision support removes these limitations by enabling the user to define business categories and key performance indicators that reflect the company's current business rules without customizing MFG/PRO. These rule-based definitions lie outside the MFG/PRO databases, preserving data integrity and increasing speed and flexibility of reporting.

Other Information

MFG/PRO software functions using a Windows GUI and a character mode user interface simultaneously are concurrently available in 26 languages.

IFS/AVALON—INDUSTRIAL AND FINANCIAL SYSTEMS

IFS (Industrial and Financial Systems) is an international company providing ERP solutions to the manufacturing community. IFS' solutions have been successfully implemented around the globe, from Fortune 500 companies to small/medium-sized enterprises.

IFS' object-oriented business solutions are built on standards. IFS' ERP software is designed with best-practice standard tools such as Oracle and Rational Rose. The component-based architecture is truly flexible, supporting not only current operations, but also the unique changes continually occurring in business.

Financials

Controlling financials. Accurately managing and tracking the financial position is critical to any manufacturing operation. With IFS financials one can support the enterprise-wide financial operation of business.

Key modules in IFS financials include:

•General Ledger •Accounts Payable •Accounts Receivable •Report Generator •Consolidated Accounts •Fixed Assets.

IFS/General ledger. The richly-functional IFS/General ledger application manages your financial data and reporting requirements through tight interfaces with other IFS financial modules and with the distribution, manufacturing, and maintenance applications.

Capabilities at a glance

•Powerful but easy-to-use report writer •Support for multiple dimensional analysis and reporting •Multiple-currency functionality •Facilitation of the budgeting process •Integrated company consolidations process for both actuals and budgets •Integrated fixed assets module •Integrated project accounting.

IFS/Accounts payable. This helps maximize the cash flow by providing tools to manage payments to suppliers.

Capabilities at a glance

•Supports various selection criteria for creating payment proposals •Handles foreign currency payments and directly converts it to accounting currency •Matches purchase receipts to invoices and payments •Supports various types of payments •Provides an easy mechanism to set-up vendors and vendor groups •Includes various standard reports and queries •Allows for offsetting against credits, prepayments, and supplier accounts receivable.

IFS/Accounts receivable. This capability helps monitor receivables and invoice and collect payments from customers.

Capabilities at a glance

•Integrated with IFS/customer order for receipt of invoicing information •Provides the ability to create invoices manually •Processes payment receipts in any currency •Supports credit memo processing •Includes various standard reports and queries.

Distribution

Customer contact is a crucial aspect of any business operation and one needs all the information possible to satisfy a variety of customer scenarios. IFS distribution allows multiple views of the customer order process giving the flexibility to deal with customers to maximum mutual benefit.

Key modules

•Customer Orders •Invoicing •Purchasing •Inventory.

Capabilities at a glance

•Tracking of raw material from acquisition from vendor to shipment of finished goods to customer •Support for multi-company, multi-warehouse, multilingual, and multi-currency operations •Availability of promise dates to customers at order time, based on material availability and plant capacity •Multiple methods of computing special pricing and discounts •User-defined order types that allow for simplified, configurable order entry by customers or customer groups •Warehouse management routines such as pallet handling, load planning, and picking zones, to facilitate efficient picking and shipping that helps ensure on-time delivery to customer.

IFS' distribution can generate purchase orders using a variety of methods, fully integrated with IFS financials. It is possible to conveniently define how an enterprise operates and avoid being locked in to some one business model.

Capabilities at a glance

•Purchase requirements can be generated via the planning system, manually, or as a result of customer orders •Statistical information about a vendor's performance, such as on-time delivery, product cost, and quality, can be generated •Services and non-stocked items are handled routinely •Delivery schedules can be developed for repetitive deliveries and blanket orders •Integration with all other IFS application modules, including IFS maintenance, is complete and seamless.

Manufacturing

With the right information available for decision-making, manufacturing complexity has given way to greater simplicity and higher efficiencies on the shop floor. Mixed-mode manufacturing allows more flexibility than ever before in keeping with customer demands. The market no longer accepts standard products with long lead times. Custom-configured products produced repetitively with just-in-time delivery are now the norm. IFS manufacturing supports the mixed-mode environment and allows to meet the competition.

It is possible to have a complete set of planning and scheduling capabilities to run simulations on material requirements planning (MRP), capacity requirements planning (CRP) or master scheduling (MS) prior to finalizing a plan. With IFS manufacturing, freedom is gained to explore different opportunities without having to disrupt the current plan.

Key modules

•Finite Scheduling •Costing •Shop Floor Reporting •Capacity Requirements Planning •Material Requirements Planning •Shop Order •Master Scheduling.

Capabilities at a glance

• Creation of master production schedule (MPS) from both forecasted demand and customer orders • Unlimited planning horizons and user-defined buckets to allow flexible formatting of planning information • Rough-cut resource planning (RRP) to allow MRP simulations before proceeding to final MRP • MPS simulation ability prior to final master schedule • Multiple planning methods for MRP • Planning by site or plant • MRP requirements fed to shop floor, purchasing, and distribution • CRP monitoring of detailed capacity for manpower and machines • Support for backward and forward scheduling • Constraint-based forward scheduling throughout the entire planning system.

Information for managing the manufacturing processes, as well as for managing industry-specific applications such as engineering, costing, and project tracking is all available within IFS manufacturing.

Additional capabilities

• Direct entry of routing information or uploading through IFS engineering to provide greater flexibility and control • Revision-level control and engineering change control standard • Ability to monitor work-in-process, time and attendance, and order status • Time and material fed directly into IFS/Costing • Product cost roll-ups, standard costs, and variance reporting standard • Through IFS/Project, the assigning of shop orders to user-defined projects for time and cost accumulation.

Whether it is a discrete, make-to-order, or mixed-mode environment, IFS manufacturing can help the plant increase productivity and efficiency. With an easy-to-use GUI environment, users will quickly become accustomed to having the right information when they need it for effective decision-making.

Resource Management

Tracking time (labour and equipment) is an integral part of any manufacturing operation. Tracking employee arrival and departure times and actual run times of work orders is a challenging task. Having to do this through different systems, manually, or by storing the data in a centralized database can be overwhelming. With these in mind, IFS has created the IFS Resource Management solution, which comprises the following modules.

Key modules

• Equipment performance • Equipment monitoring • Shop floor reporting • Skills and certification • Payroll interface • Time management •Time and attendance •Accounting rules •Document management.

Providing selectability of the most-needed modules and an easy-to-understand GUI, IFS Resource Management is not just an application, but a total solution. A particularly troublesome issue is employee time tracking. Having to involve the payroll and human resource departments in day-to-day work time, vacation, and sick leave tracking can add up to unnecessarily costly expense. IFS/Time and Attendance can help reduce much of that expense.

Capabilities at a glance

•Interactive "RegTime" terminals equipped with 4" displays allow easy data entry from the office or shop floor •RegTime terminals allow customization of messages and instructions •Employees can receive instant feedback regarding time issues •Rule-based for a truly flexible, data-driven rule engine for time (absence/presence) classification, flex codes, etc •Programmable interface to third party payroll and manufacturing solutions.

Tracking, reviewing, and correcting stop times in capital equipment and recording piece counts for shifts in the operation can be tedious. Capturing this data through IFS/Equipment monitoring and IFS/Shop floor reporting helps you manage and minimize errors.

Additional capabilities

•Ability to gather data from PLC's or by manual entry from the shop floor •Accurate, real-time information about machine production time, idle time, manufactured quantities, and events •Time and frequency counting on 20 custom-specific shutdown reasons •User definition of sub-codes at every stop reason •Quantity counting can be accomplished in various ways and can be enabled or disabled for each activity reason •Receipt of real-time status, shift and order-information updates on demand.

Maintenance

Breakdowns and repair delays can be a nightmare for today's maintenance managers. IFS maintenance has a proven and complete maintenance management solution to help reduce downtime. This family of modules helps make the maintenance system more adaptable and responsive to constantly changing conditions. This module helps realize increased equipment efficiency and consequently, an improved bottom line.

Key modules

•Work Order •Preventive Maintenance •Scheduling •Equipment •Inventory •Purchasing.

Capabilities at a glance

•Flexible maintenance scheduling for preventive, predictable, and corrective maintenance tasks •Interfaces with real-time production data •Complete visibility into spare parts inventory for issuing purchase orders on demand •Revision planning based on user-definable priorities •Integrated statistical control for maximizing productivity and overall equipment efficiency •Enterprise-wide accounting rules to facilitate consistency in all financial maintenance transactions •Manual and electronic document management links to work orders as well as to all types of maintenance objects •Cradle-to-grave component tracking with multi-level physical structures •Critical event notification through pager calls and E-mail messaging •Remote access via Internet •Bar code capabilities •Facilitation of increase in operational safety.

Engineering

For manufacturing enterprises that have a need for heavily engineered products, IFS engineering contains several modules to help them address the critical engineering, documentation management, and project needs.

Key modules

•Project •Project Delivery •PDM (Product Data Management) •Document Management.

Capabilities at a glance

•Stores all construction and configuration information about a part •Manages and secures all data relevant to the development process •Maintains complete engineering change orders and control (ECN, ECO) records for each product, from conception to manufacture •Helps increase efficiency, quality, and standardization of products and processes •Controls distribution of documents to different subscribers •Ensures through revision control that the correct version of the document is always used in links to other IFS applications •Provides complete document archiving •Reduces time and expense throughout the operation of the enterprise.

To better organize projects and track project costs, IFS/Project and IFS/Project delivery modules, give the visibility of the project's status and act as a powerful solution to automatically handle the project management needs.

Additional capabilities

• Caters to user-definable projects • Handles sub-projects and tasks within projects • Permits planning and cost accumulation at any level, from a partial roll-up to the total project • Shop- and purchase orders can be tied to specific projects • Provides budgeting by project • Provides detailed analysis of dynamic activities such as per cent completion and costs to date • Posts all transactions automatically to the correct general ledger accounts • Allows project number to be one of many segments within the chart of accounts • IFS/Project delivery provides guidelines and information to enable successful implementation of any project within the user organization.

A formalized approach to improving efficiency and costs throughout the enterprise starts with engineering and spreads across the whole organization and IFS Engineering provides the tools to improve effectiveness. As a result, the needed level of detailed control can be maintained and simultaneously, the right information can be conveyed to the rest of the organization.

BAAN IV

The Baan Company is a leading provider of enterprise and inter-enterprise business software solutions. The company's family of products is designed to help corporations maintain a competitive advantage in the management of critical business processes by means of a product architecture that lends itself to fast implementations and ease of change.

Baan IV is an integrated family of manufacturing, distribution, finance and transportation, service, project and orgware modules. The solution offers a new concept in business management software that incorporates and goes beyond ERP. Using the principle of **dynamic enterprise modelling (DEM)** implemented via its Orgware capabilities, Baan IV enables a company to match its specific business processes and organization model with the extensive functionality of the Baan applications. Baan IV is specially designed to meet the needs of key vertical markets. Furthermore, Baan also extends supply chain support beyond the boundaries of an organization to support trading partner management as well.

Baan IV provides a scalable architecture making it possible for all enterprises—Fortune 500, mid-size or small-scale to cost-effectively implement the Baan software. Baan IV has a client-server architecture, runs on most popular environments and is Internet-enabled to provide customers with the operational flexibility they need to be the leaders in their marketplace.

About Baan

The Baan Company is a worldwide leader in enterprise-wide business software applications and consulting services for companies in the hybrid manufacturing, automotive, electronics, process, and heavy equipment and project services industries. Its corporate mission is to provide companies with innovative business software solutions which are aligned with a company's organizational structure, business practices, and operational procedures.

The Baan Company was founded in 1978 in Ede by Jan Baan, an early advocate of open systems technology and concurrent engineering. Baan now operates from dual corporate headquarters in Putten, the Netherlands and Menlo Park, California. Today, the company has more than 3,000 employees worldwide who contribute to an extensive corporate knowledge of manufacturing environments and open systems technology. Since 1978, Baan has experienced several major events.

The company offers the Baan family of UNIX and NT-based, client/server enterprise business solutions which are Year 2000 compliant and support the entire spectrum of an organization's business processes, including manufacturing, finance, distribution, and service and maintenance operations. In addition, Baan offers Orgware, a suite of organizational tools and software utilities that helps reduce the time and cost of implementation and continuous improvement. With Orgware, its key differentiator, Baan enables dynamic enterprise modelling, a new paradigm which delivers a framework for insuring that enterprise applications are in close alignment with changing processes and business models.

Leading organizations worldwide have adopted Baan's customer-driven approach to achieve corporate objectives of improving profitability, productivity and lead-times. With over 4,000 customer sites worldwide, Baan customers include global leaders in manufacturing, such as ABB, Boeing, Mercedes-Benz, Nortel, Philips and Snap-on Incorporated.

The Baan family of business software solutions comprises applications, tools and Orgware that work together as a fully integrated system, supporting all aspects of a business. The applications provide customers with support for multiple languages and currencies.

Baan has three international services centres, located in the United States, The Netherlands, and India. These provide product training, implementation assistance, and systems and applications consulting. The centres work with Baan alliance partners and customers to transfer applications knowledge to end-users to ensure that customers meet their operational goals.

Applications

Baan's applications support a fully integrated, hybrid manufacturing environment, offering integrated applications that address the spectrum of manufacturing scenarios, like make-to-stock, assemble-to-order, make-to-order and engineer-to-order.

Baan manufacturing. This includes multi-site MRP, product configuration, project control and critical path activity analysis capabilities. It manages repetitive and job shop production and supply chain control for multi-site manufacturing.

Baan distribution and transportation. This section manages sales and purchasing, with order processing, margin monitoring and contract administration capabilities. Additionally, this module offers comprehensive functionality for external logistics and transportation, providing route optimization, transport order management, transport maintenance, and public warehousing and packaging. It can be tightly integrated with Baan's EDI module, enabling rapid communication with clients and subcontractors.

Baan finance. It is a complete, integrated financial system that provides General Ledger, Fixed Assets, Accounts Payable and Accounts Receivable capabilities. It can be used as an integrated portion of a complete Baan solution or in a standalone mode for companies that only require the financial management capabilities.

Baan service. It offers installation control, contract control, service order control and invoicing.

Baan project. This is designed for the manufacturing and construction industries, and supports the management of large projects through all stages, from estimating tenders to delivery and throughout the guarantee period.

Baan process. This process delivers the key functionality required for process manufacturers, including formulation and co-product/by-product management fully integrated with discrete ERP for hybrid environments.

Baan tools. Baan tools is a powerful 4GL application development environment that provides end-users a fast, easy way to tailor Baan applications to achieve custom implementation. Baan Tools' open architecture enables users to develop applications that are easily and seamlessly portable across multiple open systems hardware platforms, operating systems, databases, user interfaces and networks. All Baan applications are developed with Baan Tools, which also is available as a separate development product.

Orgware. Baan supports its customers with a comprehensive set of pre-sales and post-sales methodologies and services delivered by Baan directly or through a growing network of alliance partners. Orgware offers customizable process models which are tightly linked to the applications to speed implementation and end-user training, enabling companies to maximize quickly their return on investment in their Baan system.

Baan Orgware comprises four components which resolve the critical business issue of mapping business systems to an organization. These include the Enterprise Modeler modelling tool, Enterprise Reference Models, Enterprise Performance Manager for benchmarking implementation success, and Enterprise Implementer, which includes tools to manage the actual implementation process.

Manufacturing

Achieving flexibility, speed, and product quality in manufacturing operations can give a definitive competitive edge in the market. Baan Manufacturing supports many types of production management strategies, such as engineer-to-order, make-to-order, assemble-to-order, and make-to-stock. For example, the Master Production Scheduling module assists business in day-to-day production control and long-term planning, and the Product Configuration module streamlines the processing of configured products.

One outstanding Baan Manufacturing feature is an approach called customer order decoupling point (CODP). This approach distinguishes different types of production so companies are able to determine the point at which production changes from standard-forecast production to customer-specific production. Combining work orders and repetitive manufacturing in the production operation and manufacturing the same product using different methods is a benefit that lets companies change methods as needs change through a product's life cycle.

Baan Manufacturing's extensive planning and scheduling capabilities translate companies' business goals into manufacturing plans. Graphical simulations allow analyzing the effect of alternative plans on financial requirements, capacity, and inventory. Because the application supports both centralized and local planning, interplant relationships can be freely defined, thus providing complete supply-chain management. In addition, the shop-floor control modules in Baan Manufacturing monitor all shop floor activity, including subcontract operations, and simplify data entry for personnel, while at the same time providing complete visibility of manufacturing activities.

Key modules

- Capacity Requirements Planning
- Engineering Change Control
- Engineering Data Management
- Master Production Scheduling

• Material Requirements Planning • Product Classification • Product Configuration • Production Control • Production Planning • Project Budgeting • Project Control • Project Network Planning • Repetitive Manufacturing.

Finance

Effective financial management is critical to business success, but a company's managers cannot manage what they cannot see. Baan Finance delivers a high level of visibility for financial transactions and drill-down capability that gives detailed transaction information online.

Baan Finance's multi-currency capabilities allow transactions in any currency; accounts and invoice balances can be revalued easily. Companies can distribute or centralize accounting functions in whatever way is most appropriate without limiting the ability to consolidate corporate information. The Activity-Based Costing module which gives information needed to gauge the cost of the different activities in business is also included.

Key modules

• Accounts Payable • Accounts Receivable • Activity-Based Costing • Budget System • Cash Management • Cost Allocation • Financial Statements • Fixed Assets • General Ledger.

Project

If a business executes customized projects for customers, comprehensive project control is undoubtedly fundamental to its profitability. With Baan Project, companies have the control needed to meet promised delivery dates and cost targets for even the most complex projects. Baan Project manages all the aspects of projects and contracts, providing visibility for all project activities and helping to ensure that delivery dates are met.

The goal of the Baan Project is cost-effective management for each project according to its particular time schedule, specified budget, and required quality. The software includes estimates and bids, scheduling, planning, budgeting, purchasing, tracking, billing, and integration into financial, manufacturing, and distribution operations. Finally, Baan Project enables companies to anticipate the impact of a project on capacity and cash flow, with the result that productivity improves and resources are used in the best manner possible.

Key modules

• Project Budget • Project Definition • Project Estimating • Project Invoicing • Project Monitoring • Project Planning • Project Progress • Project Requirements Planning.

Distribution and Transportation

Baan distribution and transportation: Strategies and tools for logistics management. Baan Transportation handles all modes of external logistics and transportation. The application includes powerful features for managing public warehousing and packaging, and offers the flexibility of easy configuration to specific requirements. In addition, Baan Transportation provides an integrated solution that is able to successfully manage both internal and external logistics.

Baan Distribution is designed to provide companies with effective distribution operations that span the globe. The application handles day-to-day logistics for manufacturers and wholesalers using sophisticated forecasting tools, comprehensive sales, purchasing, inventory management, and extensive distribution planning and transportation management. Baan Distribution's **electronic data interchange (EDI)** speeds up communications between businesses while fostering closer trading-partner relationships. The application also supports multiple distribution planning strategies that provide a solid link between distribution operations and manufacturing planning.

Key modules

•Distribution Requirements Planning •Electronic Data Interchange (EDI) •HIFS's and Expense Control •Inventory Location Control •Invoicing •Lot Control •Packing Control •Public Warehousing •Purchase Contracts •Purchase Control •Purchase Inquiries •Sales Contracts •Sales Control •Sales and Marketing Information •Sales Quotations •Replenishment Order Control •Transportation Fleet Management •Transportation Fuel Control •Transportation Order Control •Transportation Order Planning •Transportation Rate Control.

SAP

Introducing SAP

SAP was founded in 1972 and has grown to become the world's fifth largest software company.

SAP is both the name of the company and the computer system. The SAP system comprises a number of fully integrated modules, which cover every aspect of business management. The system has been developed to meet the increasing needs of commercial and other organizations that are striving for greater efficiency and effectiveness. While many software companies have looked at areas of business and developed systems to support those areas, SAP has looked toward the whole business. They offer a unique system that supports nearly all areas of business on a global scale. SAP provides the opportunity to replace large numbers of independent systems that have been developed and implemented in established organizations with one single modular system. Each module performs a different function, but is designed to work with other modules. It is fully integrated, offering true compatibility across business functions.

SAP is a German company but operates all over the world, with 28 subsidiaries and affiliates and six partner companies maintaining offices in 40 countries.

SAP's Markets

SAP markets its products all over the world to almost every industry imaginable, as well as to government and educational institutions and hospitals. The following is a list of industries served by SAP:

- Raw materials, mining and agriculture
- Oil and gas
- Chemical
- Pharmaceuticals
- Building materials, clay and glass
- Building and heavy construction
- Primary metals, metal products, steel
- Industrial and commercial machinery
- Automotive industry
- Ship-building, aerospace, and train construction
- Transportation services and tourism
- Electronic/optic and communication equipment
- Wood and paper
- Furniture
- Consumer packaged goods—foods
- Clothing and textiles
- Retail and wholesale trading
- Communication services and media
- Storage, distribution and shipping
- Utilities
- Financial services, banks and insurance
- Government, public administration, and services

- Museums and associations
- Health care and hospitals
- Educational institutions and research
- Consulting and software
- Services.

SAP R/3 APPLICATIONS

Financials

SAP's suite of integrated financial application components encompasses all aspects of financial accounting, investment management, control, treasury management, and enterprise control. Accounting lies at the core of an enterprise. SAP's R/3 system improves the bottom line by letting it interpret and work with financial data more effectively than before.

Financial accounting. Company-wide control and integration of financial information is essential to strategic decision-making. R/3 Financial Accounting gives the ability to centrally track financial accounting data within an international framework of multiple companies, languages, currencies, and charts of accounts. For example, when raw materials move from inventory into manufacturing, the system reduces quantity values in inventory and simultaneously subtracts dollar values for inventory accounts in the balance sheet.

The Financial Accounting component complies with international accounting standards such as GAAP and IAS. It also fulfills the local legal requirements of many countries and reflects fully the legal and accounting changes resulting from European market and currency unification. Although R/3 Financial Accounting transactions are processed individually, they are integrated with all other relevant financial areas.

General ledger. R/3 general ledger (GL) is essential both to the financial accounting system and to strategic decision-making. Through active integration with business processes in R/3 logistics and in the accounting subledgers, R/3 GL serves as a central pool of financial data for financial reporting as well as for other accounting areas. The GL supports all the functions needed in a financial accounting system. This includes flexible structuring of the chart of accounts at group and company level, distributed application scenarios using Application Link Enabling (ALE), real-time simultaneous update of subledgers and the general ledger, elimination of time-consuming reconciliation, and parallel views of data in both the general ledger and managerial accounting applications.

As an enhancement to the GL, the Special Purpose Ledger system provides summary information from other components at a user-defined level of detail. By creating combinations of entered data, you generate data summaries that can be used in planning, allocation, distribution, and reporting.

R/3's Special Purpose Ledger also allows taking advantage of more functions in GL and in Cost Centre Accounting. For example, you can create your own database tables and define non-standard fields to suit specialized accounting or reporting requirements.

Accounts receivable and payable. R/3 offers a financial overview of global business partner relationships in the Accounts Receivable and Payable subledger functions. These subledgers are integrated both with the GL and with areas in R/3 sales and distribution (SD) and materials management (MM), where financial data originates. Accounts Receivable and Payable transactions are performed automatically when related processes take place in other R/3 components.

This module uses standard business rules for procedures ranging from data entry and reporting to processing payments and bank transactions. Accounts Receivable and Payable functions include Internet integration; document management; full support for EDI processing, including automatic clearing by lockbox processing; integration with cash management, and flexible reporting using customer and vendor information systems. The module also provides flexible dunning, enterprise-wide credit management with workflow integration, payment automation with EFT and check processing, and document parking with various approval procedures.

Fixed asset accounting. R/3 Asset Accounting manages the company's fixed assets. Within the Financial Accounting system, FI-AA serves as a subledger to the General Ledger, providing detailed information on asset-related transactions. Significant features include country-specific charts of depreciation complying with local legal requirements, full support throughout the asset life cycle from acquisition to retirement, depreciation simulation and interest calculation, and integration with project management and order accounting for management of capital assets. Asset Accounting also provides integration with plant maintenance for management of machinery and equipment, management of leased assets and assets under construction, mass processing with workflow integration, and interactive reporting.

Legal consolidation. Consolidated financial statements need to be integrated effectively with operational data at the individual company level. Using different valuation methods, one can plan balance sheet strategies to suit typical requirements.

R/3 Legal Consolidation (FI-LC) is closely linked to the Financial Accounting system, permitting direct data transfer from individual statements into the consolidated report. In addition to the consolidated statements required by law, Legal Consolidation also allows the creation of multiple views of consolidation data. With these views you can generate reports about legal entities or segments of business.

Controlling

Overhead cost control. Many organizations experience a significant increase in the percentage of indirect costs which cannot be directly assigned to the products manufactured or services rendered. While cost monitoring and optimization may be quite advanced in production areas, transparency is often lacking in overhead cost areas. The Overhead Cost Controlling (CO-OM) component focuses on monitoring and allocation of overheads.

Cost centre accounting. Cost Centre Accounting (CO-OM-CCA) analyzes where overhead occurs within the organization. Costs are assigned to the sub-areas of the organization where they originated. The R/3 system offers a wide variety of methods for allocating posted amounts and quantities. In particular, activity accounting permits the allocation of costs to products based on cost sources, enabling assignments which were not previously possible.

Overhead orders. Overhead Orders (CO-OM-OPA) collects and analyzes costs based on individual internal measures. The R/3 system can monitor and automatically check budgets assigned to each measure.

Activity-based costing. Activity-Based Costing (CO-OM-ABC) is developed as the response to the growing need for monitoring and control of cross-departmental business processes in addition to functions and products. Organizational transparency in overhead areas is substantially enhanced by seeing costs in a new light. The R/3 system automatically determines the utilization of business processes by products, customers, and other cost objects based on the cost drivers taken from the integrated accounting environment.

Product cost control. Product Cost Control (CO-PC) determines the costs arising from manufacturing a product or providing a service. Plan and standard values serve in evaluating warehouse stock and for contrasting revenues received with costs. In addition, the values in Product Cost Controlling are crucial for determining the lowest price limit for which a product is profitable. Simulations illustrate the effects of changes in production methods on the cost of goods manufactured.

Cost object controlling. Cost Object Controlling (CO-PC-OBJ) helps to monitor manufacturing orders. Integration with the R/3 Logistics components results in a logistical quantity flow that provides instant information on actual cost, object costs, allowing ongoing costing calculations at any time. Follow-up calculations determine and analyze the variances between actual manufacturing costs and the plan costs resulting from Product Cost Planning. In addition, the R/3 system can evaluate work in process and post the results to Financial Accounting.

Profitability analysis. Profitability Analysis (CO-PA) examines the sources of returns. As part of sales control, Profitability Analysis is the last step in cost-based settlement, where revenues are assigned to costs according to market segment. You can define any market segment—distinguishing, for example, between products, customers, orders, sales organizations, distribution channels, and business areas—and evaluate it according to contribution and revenue margins. Information from Profitability Analysis frames important decisions in areas such as determining prices, selecting customers, developing conditions, and choosing distribution channels.

Investment management

Corporation-wide budgeting. R/3 Investment Management facilitates investment planning and budgeting at a level higher than specific orders or projects. As a result of subsequently assigning the specific investment measures (internal orders or projects) to positions in the hierarchy, you are kept up-to-date about available funds, planned costs, and actual costs already incurred from internal and external activities. The investment program allows you to distribute budgets which are used during the capital spending process. The system helps to monitor, and thereby avoid, budget overruns.

Appropriation requests. R/3 IM provides tools to plan and manage your capital spending projects starting at their earliest stages. In the initial stage of the capital spending process, you enter the application for the spending project as an appropriation request. You define your own evaluation and approval process, during which the system keeps a detailed history of the status of the appropriation request. You transfer the data from the appropriation request to the investment measure when the request is approved for implementation. You enter detailed plan values in the appropriation request, and its different variants, for use in the pre-investment analysis.

Investment measures. Depending on their complexity, investment measures that need to be monitored individually can be represented either as internal orders or as projects. These internal orders or projects provide the means for actually carrying out the capital investment; that is, they serve as the objects for collecting primary and secondary costs, for calculating overhead and interest, for managing down payments and commitments, and for handling other related tasks. As the result of having an asset under construction assigned to it, the investment measure also benefits from all of the required asset accounting functions. Settlement is both flexible and almost fully automatic. This kind of settlement ensures complete integration with business planning and control, and provides consistently up-to-date values.

Automatic settlement to fixed assets. R/3 IM recognizes the importance of the asset accounting aspects of investment measures. The system automatically separates costs requiring capitalization from costs that are not capitalized, debiting the correct costs to the asset under construction. For different accounting needs, the system can use different capitalization rules for making this split. At completion, the investment measure can be settled to various receivers by line item. Asset accounting provides precise proof of origin for all transactions affecting acquisition and production costs.

Depreciation forecast. R/3 IM budgeted balance sheets and cost planning are always based on current values. Planned depreciation values for investment measures and appropriation requests can be transferred directly to ongoing overhead cost planning. The system recalculates expected depreciation amounts whenever planning data is updated.

Treasury

Cash management. The Cash Management component allows the analysis of financial transactions for a given period. Cash Management also identifies and records future developments for the purposes of financial budgeting. In R/3 Treasury Cash Management (TCM), the company's payment transactions are grouped into cash holdings, cash inflows, and cash outflows. Cash Management provides information on the sources and uses of funds to secure liquidity to meet payment obligations when they become due.

Cash Management also monitors and controls incoming and outgoing payment flows, and supplies the data required for managing short-term money market investments and borrowing. Depending on the time period under review, a distinction is made between cash position, short-term cash management and medium- and long-term financial budgeting.

SAP's R/3 Cash Management component thus ensures that all information relevant to liquidity is available for analysis purposes, creating a basis for the necessary cash management decisions. In bank account management, electronic banking and control functions provide support for managing and monitoring of bank accounts. Besides the liquidity forecast function integrates anticipated payment flows from financial accounting, purchasing, and sales to create a liquidity outlook for the medium to long-term.

The cash position and liquidity forecast components generally cover both foreign currency holdings and expected foreign currency items.

Treasury management. In your role as treasurer, you take the results of your current liquidity, currency, and risk positions and consider the conditions prevailing on the money and capital markets before implementing concrete decisions in the form of financial instruments in Treasury Management. The Treasury Management component offers functions for managing financial deals and positions, from trading through to transferring data to Financial Accounting. Treasury Management also supports flexible reporting and evaluation structures for analyzing financial deals, positions, and portfolios.

For short-term liquidity and risk management, one can use money market or foreign exchange transactions to smooth out liquidity squeezes and gluts or to eliminate currency risks. Securities and loans come into play in the medium- and long-term.

Active management of interest rate and currency risks is facilitated by derivative financial instruments. The trading area contains functions for recording financial deals, exercising rights, performing evaluations, and calculating prices (for example, option price calculator). In back-office processing, you enter the additional data required for processing deals (such as account assignment and payment details) and generate automatic confirmations. Position management functions, such as securities account transfers or corporate actions relating to securities, are also supported in the back office area. The general ledger is updated in the accounting area, which also offers flexible payment processing functions in addition to valuation and accrual/deferral methods. By using common organizational elements throughout, various organizational structures can be represented in the system, such as a central enterprise-wide treasury department or "in-house banks". This also ensures full integration of Treasury into other SAP R/3 components.

Market risk management. Market Risk Management plays a vital role within Treasury in ensuring the company's competitiveness. The process involves a complex feedback loop encompassing data collection, risk measurement, analysis, and simulation as well as active planning of financial instruments. This process dovetails closely into other treasury and corporate functions. To reduce the complexity of this management process, a powerful set of management tools is required.

Market Risk Management acts as an integrated, central risk control station with monitoring and management functions. Access to information on current and future cash flows and on financial deals already processed is an absolute must. As a result, Cash Management, which pools all cash flows from the business sectors such as sales and distribution or purchasing, forms the basis. Consequently, all cash flows from the company's operating business can be accessed for the purposes of risk management. Furthermore, all financial transactions managed in Treasury Management can be evaluated together with the cash flows generated by the various operating divisions.

The component provides various measurements for analyzing and assessing interest rate and currency risks. Market-to-market, effective rate and effective yield calculations are based on up-to-the-minute market data, uploaded via data feed, and financial transactions or positions. By simulating market data, you can determine the risk structure of "what-if" analyses (such as crash scenarios or worst case scenarios). You can also measure and compare the impact of alternative hedging strategies using simulated transactions.

Funds management. R/3 Funds Management (TR-FM) supports the funds management process from budgeting all the way through to payments, including monitoring expenditures, activities, resources, and revenues.

Budgeting in TR-FM offers many useful functions. From original budget through approval and release, to budget supplements, returns, and transfers, you will find support for all stages of the budgeting process. Budgets are entered for areas of responsibility which can cover as many management levels as required. Fund centres and their hierarchical structure provide a base for top-down budgeting and represent responsibility areas within budget control. The Commitment Management System enables you to control your various funds commitments and determine how much of the budget has already been utilized via availability checking. The information system can supply information at any time on when, where, and how the funds commitments arose. Analyses by responsibility area and commitment items allow identification of any budget bottlenecks.

With release 4.0, the SAP R/3 module enterprise controlling (EC) will help you to reinvent your corporate reporting. It will help to save time and money in preparing reliable up-to-date business information by automating all the time-consuming tasks. EC actually consists of three components: EC-EIS Executive Information System, EC-CS Consolidation and EC-PCA Profit Centre Accounting.

IEM (Integrated Enterprise Management) with EC (Enterprise Controlling). Getting accounting data prepared by subsidiaries for corporate reporting will be automatically prepared simultaneously within the local books of each subsidiary. It is easy to transfer that data to the EC module to automatically set up consolidated financial statements including elimination of intercompany transactions, currency translation, etc. EC-CS Consolidation is the first available standard software component for financial statutory and management consolidation, which also allows fully automated consolidation of investments—even for many companies and complex investment structures.

EC-PCA (Profit Centre Accounting) 4.0 allows you to work with internal transfer prices and at the same time to have the right values from company, profit centre and enterprise perspectives in parallel. Any transaction in R/3, which touches an object such as customer order, plant or cost centre allocated to a profit centre will be automatically posted to EC-PCA. Furthermore, you can directly take data from EC-PCA to EC-CS Consolidation to prepare complete financial statutory statements and management reports in parallel. This provides the management with a consistent view of external and internal financial management reports.

EC-EIS (Executive Information System) allows you to take financial data from EC-PCA, EC-CS or indeed any other R/3 application and combine it with external data (market data, industry benchmarks) and/or data from non-SAP applications to build a company-specific comprehensive enterprise information system which can serve as a self-service 'business cockpit' for managers and executives.

EC (Enterprise Controlling) allows you to control the enterprise from a corporate and a business unit perspective within one common infrastructure (within one or several R/3 EC systems). It helps to speed up provision of business control information by fully automated corporate reporting from operative accounting via financial consolidation to management reporting. From EC-EIS top-level reports, end users can drill-down to more detailed information within EC or any other R/3 application. Even all companies are not using R/3 it does not present a problem because EC can work with data from SAP and non-SAP sources.

Logistics applications always work hand in hand to help improve the supply chain. All functions of these applications are planned, controlled and coordinated within the system across all organizational units. Since the R/3 system automatically links all the elements that logically belong together, no work is duplicated. You only need to enter data once. In the R/3 system, the processes involved in logistics, financials, and human resources are harmonized with one another, opening up a new dimension of business efficiency.

PDM (Product Data Management)

PDM supports in creating and managing product data throughout the product life cycle. SAP supports two basic scenarios in the PDM environment. You can choose whether to connect a third party PDM system supported by SAP's Complementary Software Program to your R/3 system, or to implement the single-source PDM solution provided within the R/3 system.

PDM keeps track of all master data. The Document Management System allows you to manage a wide range of technical, commercial, and administrative documents consistently. You can link original documents to all types of objects in the R/3 system (for example, material master records, BOMs, or change master records). You can also access external optical archiving systems.

PDM organizes the design and change processes. One of the most important features of Engineering Change Management is full integration in the logistics process chain of a company. Engineering Change Management ensures that planned changes to master data are automatically available in the productive functions of sales and distribution, demand management and MRP, production control, product costing, quality management, and materials management at any given time.

PDM gives the product structure information at a glance. BOM Management finally solves the problem of distinguishing between engineering BOMs and production BOMs in your company. To maintain the distinction between the different uses of a BOM, you can either create entirely separate BOMs or define different views on the same BOM. PDM functions are also supported for large product development projects in the R/3 Project System.

Sales and distribution. The R/3 System's Sales and Distribution application offers access to real-time, online information from sales support to the billing process.

The Sales Support component provides you with easy-to-use tools to manage information on sales leads, sales calls, inquiries, quotations, marketing campaigns, competitors, and their products. Sales and marketing personnel can access this data at any time to perform sales activities or carry out direct mailings. You can use Sales Support not only to make your sales process more efficient and boost service to existing customers, but to identify new sources of business as well.

Order entry in the R/3 system is highly automatic. By referring to information that you enter in the simple user interface, the system assembles information, such as the terms of payment and the identity of the delivering plant. It then programmes this information in the sales order. The R/3 system deals just as easily with materials. You can enter materials manually, select from customer-based product proposals, or work with variant configurations to configure a product to meet customer requirements.

Pricing is carried out automatically in the sales order. To determine relevant predefined prices, surcharges, and discounts, the system works from price lists and customer agreements, or it determines an amount according to the product, product group, or product cost. The pricing function is very flexible and can manage even the most complicated price structures. You can maintain pricing information with data from sales deals and promotions as well.

The system also carries out a dynamic credit limit check, checking against credit, financial, and sales data to verify the customer's credit limit. You can set the system to automatically alert credit or sales personnel when a sales order fails the check.

The availability check is just as comprehensive. Run in connection with the Materials Management (MM) and Production Planning (PP) applications, it verifies that you have sufficient quantities on the requested delivery date to satisfy a sales order. If you cannot meet the requested delivery date, the system immediately determines when the desired quantity will become available so that you can instantly quote a new date to your customer. You can also review availability in multiple locations. In the case of customers requiring specific quantities of a product, you can use the make-to-order production features in the Sales and Distribution component.

Sales and Distribution supports a wide range of contracts, from the general to the more specific rental contracts. With them, you can specify delivery quantities, delivery dates, and prices. Scheduling agreements and more complex requirements such as just-in-time delivery schedules are also supported. Or, you can follow up on your products with the Service Management component which includes a complete suite of customer service functions, including call management, warranty management, service and maintenance contract processing.

Shipping Management offers easy-to-use functions for managing picking, packing, and loading tasks, and monitoring delivery deadlines. The system provides a list of all sales orders due for delivery, and gives you the option of delivering the order completely or partially, individually or collectively. At the same time, you can initiate picking for the available quantities with full integration to the Warehouse Management System.

The Transportation module offers functions for transportation planning and processing, as well as monitoring and controlling functions. No matter where you send your products by land, by air, by sea: you can represent the transportation chain in the R/3 system for individual shipments or stop-off shipments involving several deliveries and several destinations. You can also select forwarding agents and track the shipments.

Sales and Distribution also provides comprehensive support for foreign trade processing, offering automated export control to determine whether you can export specific products to a particular country, to a particular customer, and at a specific time. The system handles all the necessary customs forms automatically. To declare your shipments of goods to the government authorities, the R/3 system collects all the data required for the declarations and creates the necessary forms. Preference agreement processing is another feature. It helps you manage the shipment of products that are eligible for customs tariff preferences, track the origin of component parts, and assign a tariff classification to materials.

On the basis of orders and deliveries, the system automatically carries out billing for all due items. The system then creates an invoice, debit memo, or credit memo for each item or collectively for several transactions. You can send a billing document directly to the customer either by mail, fax, or EDI. At the same time, revenues and receivables are immediately visible in the Financial Accounting (FI) and Controlling (CO) components. It can also process rebates based on a customer's purchase volume.

SAP offers the best possible support to decision-makers in the form of its Sales Information System. As soon as you enter a Sales and Distribution document into the system, the relevant information is updated. This ensures that the information you access is always up-to-date. The information is displayed by customer, material, or region, in an easy-to-interpret list or informative graphic. By using the Sales Information System, you are in a strategic position to address market trends and changes.

Production planning and control. Equipped with the R/3 system's Production Planning and Control application, you can reach your full potential when planning, executing, and controlling production. The R/3 System's Production Planning and Control application covers the complete production process from the creation of master data to production planning, MRP, and capacity planning, right down to production control and costing.

Production planning modules. Using Sales and Operations Planning (SOP), you can create realistic and consistent planning figures and datas on the basis of expected sales or other key figures of your choice. Then, in Demand Management, these planning figures are split down to product level and the demand program is created. In material requirements planning (MRP), the system calculates the quantities and procurement dates for the necessary materials, right down to the raw materials. You can plan capacities ahead at this planning phase. Therefore, you can recognize possible capacity bottlenecks in good time to take the necessary preventive measures.

Production control modules. Depending on the method of production, you have the choice of using Production Order Processing, Repetitive Manufacturing, or KANBAN Production Control.

The production order is primarily a tool for discrete, job-shop production. It provides extensive status management functions, controlling per-order as well as various operation-related functions. Repetitive manufacturing is especially designed for manufacturers of products that are typically produced repetitively on a particular production line over a longer period. Here, production planning and control as well as controlling are usually carried out based on periods and quantities. R/3's Repetitive Manufacturing module provides a tool based on production rates and lines to cover the requirements of this type of production.

Capacity planning is integrated with production order processing as well as with repetitive manufacturing. Various dispatching strategies and a flexible graphic-planning table support you in planning your resources. If your control production using KANBAN techniques, replenishment or the production of a material is not triggered until a higher production level actually requires the material. In R/3's KANBAN module, various replenishment strategies are available for in-house production, external procurement, and stock transfer. The signal for replenishing a material can be triggered by bar code or using a graphic KANBAN board.

Quality management interfaces to PDC systems, distributed control systems, laboratory information systems as well as extensive data analysis functions in the Open Information Warehouse are all also integrated in R/3's Production Control.

Production planning covers the complete production process from the creation of master data to production planning, MRP, and capacity planning right down to production control and costing. It can be used in all sectors of industry and provides a whole range of production methods from make-to-order production/variant processing to repetitive manufacturing/mass production. The PP application provides you with tools, which guarantee a high performance level planning and control of the complete material flow in your production processes. It also provides you with easy-to-use information systems that you can adjust to suit your own particular needs. As a result, planners, work schedulers, and production schedulers are relieved of routine tasks, and therefore, have more time to concentrate on the business-critical activities.

Project system. Project objects and the business areas involved form a multifaceted network, of which project management is one part. The R/3 Project System matches this network of relationships by permitting any link you need between project management and commercial information processing. Project planning and control become an integral part of your business organization and management regimes. The comprehensive functions available in the R/3 system guarantee reliable support during all phases of an undertaking and meet the requirements typical of all types of simple as well as complex projects.

Work breakdown structures can use the project system in many different areas, such as:

•Investment management •Marketing •Software and consulting services •Research and development •Maintenance tasks

• Shutdown planning • Plant engineering and construction
• Complex make-to-order production.

The central structures in the Project system are work breakdown structures (WBS) and networks, with their attendant activities and milestones. You can also use these structures in conjunction with sales orders for sales and distribution and with BOMs for production and procurement, to model complex projects in the system.

Project system's graphical interface can be used to create structures quickly and easily. Cost and schedule planning becomes more refined as the project becomes more detailed. Integration with other modules in the R/3 system enables, for example, planning of resources in cooperation with Purchasing, Inventory, Management, and Material Requirements Planning. You can assign human resources in individual employee or group terms. The Project system checks and monitors availability of funds, capacities, and materials, ensuring that there is enough of each for the project to be carried out. You can restrict and control project expenditure using the tools for approving and releasing project budgets.

SAP Business Workflow is available to improve communications within large projects. For example, Workflow can be used to ensure that the purchasing department is immediately notified of any changes in schedule or quantity requirements.

Project information system. Throughout project processing, the system offers a flexible, high-performance information system, which makes possible the tailoring of the degree of detail of reports to suit requirements. Listings and graphical analyses supply all the information needed on the budget, planned and actual costs, revenues, commitments, schedules of payments received and made, and resources. Standard interfaces provide the two-way communications base required for further planning and calculations in additional systems and at local level.

Materials Management

The efficiency of business processes for procuring raw materials and the effectiveness of the logistics pipeline through which materials flow are factors crucial to corporate success. The R/3 System's Materials Management application not only contains all the functions required to simplify business processes in Requirements Planning, Purchasing, Inventory Management, Warehouse Management, and Invoice Verification, but also introduces a high degree of automation into standard procedures. All functions are closely integrated with each other and with other functions in R/3.

Purchasing. Consumption-based planning provides one with up-to-the-minute order proposals for purchase requisitions, based either on reorder levels or on forecast data. Logistics applications, such as Sales and Distribution, Plant Maintenance, Production Planning, or the Project System, can also require materials or services to be procured externally. Individual departments can enter purchase requisitions manually.

The system passes these purchase requisitions directly to Purchasing, where they are converted into purchase orders. Your buyers have at their command a wide array of sophisticated tools, from special purchasing master data and requests for quotations, to quotations and outline agreements. You can, for example, compare prices during the procurement process or automate the vendor selection or order creation processes. The Vendor Evaluation application enables you to find the best vendors using criteria of choice. They also have the option of requiring purchasing documents to be part of a release and approval procedure before they can be further processed. Authorized members of staff approve purchasing activities by electronic signature. You can send purchase orders or forecast delivery schedules to the vendors either on paper or electronically (by EDI, for example). The purchase order history allows you to monitor the status of your order and track deliveries or invoices already received.

Inventory management. The stock of your materials is managed on a value and quantity basis in Inventory Management. This application component supports all the most common types of receipts, issues, and stock transfers and allows you to manage special stocks (such as batches, consignment stocks, project stock, returnable transport packaging, or components with a subcontractor). Goods movements postings automatically result in an update of values in Financial Accounting, Asset Accounting, and Controlling. The system also supports a number of convenient aids for entering data and with a variety of inventory valuation methods, such as LIFO (Last in First out) or FIFO (First in First out), for balance sheet valuation.

Warehouse management. The Warehouse Management (WM) module provides flexible, automated support that enables you to process goods movements and maintains a current record of all materials stored in highly complex warehousing structures. Using advanced putaway and picking techniques, WM optimizes material flow and capacity in the warehouse, storing goods in the most favourable locations so that they are readily available when needed. The capability of WM to be interfaced to hand-held terminals, bar-code scanners, and automated warehousing systems complements the many automatic processes already available in the WM component.

Invoice verification. Invoices you receive on paper or by EDI are checked automatically in the system. If you enter an invoice referencing a purchase order, the system can automatically generate the invoice it expects to receive. An invoice is automatically blocked for payments if variances occur that are not allowed such as in the delivery date, the quantity delivered, or the agreed price.

The Evaluated Receipt Settlement (ERS) functionality allows you to do away with vendor invoices altogether. The system automatically creates invoices periodically based on the goods receipts posted in the system for purchase orders.

Invoice Verification provides a special method of entering vendor invoices, which is much faster than standard procedures.

The MM application comprises countless additional functions that can help shape the materials management system efficiently. A pipeline material that flows directly into the production process can be entered in the system for an order, a cost centre, or a network and is managed in a manner similar to consignment stock. You can use the stock transfer function to model stock movements among different plants in the system. You also have the option of entering stock transport orders with or without a purchase order or delivery. Transportation activities are made easy with a whole suite of functions, such as shipping point determination and route determination. And to ensure smooth and efficient foreign trade processing, you can quickly prepare the necessary data (for customs declarations, for example) for export or import activities.

Inventory control. With the Purchasing Information System, all the facts and figures necessary for negotiating with vendors are at hand. Choosing which data is to be included in reports and how the information has to be presented becomes easy. You can, for example, determine stock values, find out inventory turnover rates, and carry out analysis. The information systems enable you to identify trends and developments, thus providing a sound basis for decision-making.

Quality management. The R/3 system's Quality Management application improves the quality of products and increases customer satisfaction. Compliance with quality management standards is an important factor in producing high-quality products. Such products promote long-lasting customer/vendor relationships, reduce expenses, and improve competitiveness. The ISO 9000 international quality standards, for example, specify that a quality management system should be integrated with all processes in an enterprise. With QM, you can achieve a high level of quality for all processes in the logistics chain. QM is tightly integrated with the other R/3 system modules, and implementing it in a logistics system provides numerous advantages compared with isolated CAQ systems.

Verification of the quality of procured goods. The purchasing department receives the latest quality scores for vendors, as well as the pertinent quality data for requests for quotations and purchase orders. In cases where product quality is critical, the quality function can release a vendor for delivery.

The control data you predefine in QM determines which materials will be inspected and posted to inspection stock (for example, to undergo a goods receipt inspection, production inspection, or source inspection). This ensures that only products conforming with the predefined quality requirements will be released for further processing.

Reduction of administrative tasks through company-wide quality planning. If you organize your quality planning activities centrally, you can make sure that the quality requirements for quality characteristics, inspection methods, and specifications will be documented and up-to-date. The integrated use of master data ensures that inspection planning activities will be consistent and efficient.

Recording of all pertinent quality data during quality inspection. In the R/3 system, an inspection lot and the corresponding inspection results document an inspection. With the recorded inspection results, you have several options. You can record the results directly in the R/3 system, transfer results by linking test or measurement equipment to the R/3 system, or transmit inspection specifications to a subsystem via a standard interface and retrieve the inspection results using the same interface. Materials can be maintained in batches on the basis of certain quality characteristics. You can use the batch characteristics defined in QM as a means of searching for batches in a delivery.

Using the comprehensive functions for quality control. The functions for Statistical Process Control (SPC) provide a means of monitoring, controlling, and improving the processes. The R/3 system supports the use of quality control charts for this purpose.

Managing problems efficiently through quality notifications. Quality notifications provide a flexible and efficient means of solving quality-related problems for products or services. You can use the quality notifications in the R/3 system to process complaints against vendors, internal problem reports, or complaints filed by customers. You can also define corrective actions (tasks), assign tasks to persons responsible, and link the processing activities to the SAP Business Workflow to help you solve a problem quickly. Through the integration of the R/3 System's Controlling (CO) application, you can easily identify all costs incurred while processing a quality notification. Finally, you can also create a quality notification on the Internet to allow your customers to interact directly with the problem management process.

Documenting the product quality using quality certificates. In addition to the shipping documents that accompany the delivery of goods to the customer, you can include a quality certificate to verify the product quality. Besides printing a quality certificate, you can also transmit a certificate by fax or your customer can retrieve the certificate via Internet. Together, the functions of the QM component in the R/3 system make up a computer-integrated quality management system (CIQ) and provide a sound basis for "Total Quality Management".

Quality management information system. As a part of the central Logistics Information System (LIS), you can use the QM Information System at different management levels to plan, monitor, evaluate, and control quality.

Plant maintenance. The various components of Plant Maintenance are Structuring technical systems, Maintenance Resource planning, Maintenance planning, Systems for technical and cost accounting data, and Maintenance information system.

Structuring technical systems. The R/3 system's PM application is a software solution that covers all maintenance tasks for a company. PM supports the planning and execution of all maintenance activities, with regard to system availability, costs, material, and personnel deployment. The openness of the R/3 system gives you many options for integrating external systems with PM, such as

- Geographical information systems
- CAD systems
- Plant data collection systems
- Systems for entering measurement and/or counter readings (SCADA).

In this way, you can create an information base that takes business, technical, and process-related criteria into consideration and makes optimized maintenance possible.

Maintenance planning. PM supports various options for structuring technical systems with its object, type, and function-related views, and enables flexible navigation. Data concerning the planning, processing, and history of maintenance tasks is documented in the system and complies with business verification requirements.

Systems for technical and cost accounting data. You can use the comprehensive catalogue system to freely define causes, activities, and maintenance tasks. All maintenance tasks, such as inspection, servicing, and repair activities, are saved in an extensive historical database. In addition to standard indicators, diverse analysis options are also available for evaluating this data.

Maintenance information system. PM provides technical and business reports and various presentation options, according to the criteria used, like organizational unit, location, execution period for the tasks, or system manufacturer. This information helps to reduce the duration and costs of plant downtimes as a result of damage, and to recognize possible weak points within the technical system in good time. It also forms the basis for defining an optimum maintenance strategy in the sense of Total Productive Maintenance (TPM) or risk optimized maintenance. The interface-free integration of Plant Maintenance in the R/3 system forms the basis for fast and efficient communication and cooperation among the different enterprise areas. PM provides a complete, industry-wide maintenance management system that considers maintenance to be an integral component of ERP. In many cases where the PM component is well established, it has fulfilled the requirements of technical and commercial enterprise areas in its role as a complete plant information system. The standard user interface and the possibility of step-by-step implementation both ensure reduced implementation times.

Service management. The Integrated Service Management System will be essential for the future. Due to the globalization of markets, worldwide competition between companies has grown. As a result of changing company objectives, customer service has increased in importance and it is now regarded as a business in its own right. Today's system infrastructure is often characterized by a lack of integration between business systems (for example, service contract management and invoicing) and the more technical systems, like installed base management and call management. It is, thus more or less impossible to make quick decisions based on service contract obligations and resource availability. The R/3 system's Service Management module, however, provides highly integrated functionality and is suitable for all types of industry.

Installed base management. Managing the customer-installed base (regardless of whether it is your own product or a competitor's), including its configuration and history, is one of the core activities in the system.

Service agreements. Long-term service agreements and/or warranty conditions are checked when a call is logged. Services described in these documents can be freely configured with characteristics such as service window, response time, service area, and so on. Pricing is determined according to options that you select.

Call management. During the call management process, logged customer calls are automatically checked against service contract commitments and warranty conditions. You can use an extensive catalogue system as well as free format data to record and codify activities, type of damage, cause of damage, etc. All service activities are stored in a comprehensive history database.

Invoicing and billing. Invoicing and billing can be performed for service contracts on a periodic basis, and also for service orders, based on time and material consumption.

Service information system. A powerful information system is also available in SM which you can adjust to suit your own particular needs.

Human Resources Management

SAP R/3 Human Resources (HR) components provide comprehensive, process-driven solutions that can address your organization's human resources needs worldwide. This global approach, which takes into consideration country and local requirements, combines all the key functions required by HR departments to provide powerful human resources solutions.

Personnel management. SAP R/3 HR includes numerous software components, which allow dealing with human resources tasks more quickly, accurately, and efficiently.

Personnel administration. This component can create a global, fully integrated HR data structure.

Recruitment management. With this function you can hire the right people with the right skills.

Travel management. The travel management module processes travel expenses effortlessly in several currencies and formats.

Benefits administration. With this function, you can add flexibility and power to the benefits programme.

Salary administration. The salary administration function simplifies the process of rewarding employees.

Personnel administration. Information is no longer owned by specific departments, but is shared by multiple entities across an organization. This package eliminates duplicate entries, reduces the chance of error, and improves data accuracy. SAP R/3 Human Resources provides a global, fully integrated data structure for the enterprise without compromising on control over individual segments of the operations.

Employee master data. SAP R/3 Human Resources is a centralized database with integration to multiple components for processing employee information. SAP provides tools to save time and help tailor the system to fit your needs. SAP R/3 HR contains "information types" for storing any desired information about your employees. You can add your own information types as well. With R/3 Human Resources, you can enter data through the time-saving "fast entry" feature, processing data in two modes—online or background. Original documents can be scanned into HR for optical storage with SAP's ArchiveLink.

HR information system (HRIS) and executive information system (EIS). Graphical information such as organization charts or employee data can be displayed using the Human Resources Information System. HRIS includes both standard and customer-defined reports. SAP has condensed vast amounts of HR information into smaller, more meaningful units of data in the Executive Information System. EIS key figures provide the organization with information in a quantified and summarized format.

Recruitment management. Reducing the cost of recruiting and hiring new employees is a challenge for the HR professional who is responsible for placing people in the right job, at the right time, and with the right skills and education. SAP has designed the Recruitment component to help meet every facet of this challenge. This component includes processes for managing open positions/requisitions, applicant screening, selection and hiring, correspondence, reporting, and cost analysis.

Open positions. Effective management of the organization's job openings helps HR recruiters, managers, and also interested candidates. The R/3 HR Recruitment component allows direct access to data stored in other components of HR including Personnel Administration, Payroll, and (personnel) Planning. These links eliminate duplication of data entry and improve productivity.

Some examples of shared data-related to job openings include position open date, location and reporting specifics, job descriptions, and skills and education requirements. This information can be used for both internal job postings and external advertisements with newspapers, magazines, colleges, or recruitment firms.

Selection and hiring. Employee and applicant qualifications have to be matched with the requirements of the job to select candidates. HR Recruitment interfaces directly with Microsoft Word for Windows to generate standard applicant letters. You can use SAP's Office Communication link to send e-mail messages to internal applicants.

SAP provides tools to analyze costs incurred during advertising and interviewing for each open position. With the HR Recruitment component, you can efficiently and effectively manage your job openings, applications and applicant data, costs, and hiring process. Once a selection has been made and an applicant has been hired, the data gathered during the recruitment process becomes new hire information. You eliminate duplicate data entry and the possible introduction of errors caused by re-entering the data.

Travel management. HR Travel Management allows the processing of a business trip from start to finish—from the initial travel request right through to posting in Financial Accounting and Controlling. This includes any subsequent corrections and all retroactive accounting requirements. Travel data can be entered by the person travelling, or by a secretary or by the relevant department, either before or after the trip. The entry of a travel request automatically generates a workflow that makes the administrator's work much easier. Business-specific, employee-specific, and country-specific trip provisions can be implemented via system settings.

Travel Management automatically calculates the tax. It also automatically processes credit card transactions for a particular trip. The receipts can be entered in any currency and include supplementary receipt information. An optical archive is available for long-term archiving of travel receipts. Travel costs can be divided into different levels (employee, trip destination, receipt). Expenses can be posted to numerous account assignment objects, for example, cost centre, order, project, or cost object, reimburse costs incurred during a trip through payroll accounting, accounts payable accounting, or by data medium exchange.

Benefits administration. The R/3 HR Benefits Administration component provides the capabilities and flexibility to effectively manage benefits programmes for diverse employee populations. Benefits Administration uses a hierarchical structure that gives you the ability and flexibility to add new programmes at any time. Benefits programmes are made up of several benefits categories. R/3 HR's Benefits Administration can maintain an unlimited number of benefits types and individual plans that are offered to your employees. With Benefits Administration you can establish benefits groups based on specific employee demographics.

Personnel cost planning. R/3 HR Organization and Planning assists you to maintain an accurate picture of the organization's structure, no matter how fast it changes. A graphical environment makes it easy to review any moves, additions, or changes in employee positions. You can also create multiple simulations for your organization as you explore the options for making adjustments in personnel. Planning features is designed to assist you to include graphical organization charts; your staffing schedules by head count, percentage, and working hours; job and work centre descriptions; and job tasks and descriptions.

Personnel costing is a strategic success factor for every company. You can take advantage of a systematic and forward-looking planning tool that considers the final effects of all personnel events. Accurately forecasting personnel costs provides your management team with a more complete cost picture to assist them in making informed decisions.

R/3 Personnel Cost Planning enables you to perform cost comparisons between target and actual personnel costs and create cost previews. You can forecast wages, salaries, and other cost elements for open and filled positions based on simulated, planned, or actual payroll figures. You can also display your results using the R/3 business graphics feature and take advantage of the standard link to Microsoft Excel and view results in a spreadsheet format. The results are transferred to SAP R/3 Cost Accounting as required.

Payroll accounting. SAP R/3 HR Payroll Accounting can fulfill today's payroll requirements and provide the flexibility to respond to your changing needs in the future.

R/3 HR Payroll Accounting addresses payroll functions from a global point of view. You can choose to centralize your payroll processing, or decentralize the data based on country or legal entities. HR Payroll Accounting gives you the options and capabilities to establish business rules without modifying your existing payroll.

Payroll processing. The R/3 Payroll Accounting date reminder feature provides you with an online tickler system that notifies you when transactions are due for processing. When the process is completed, a built-in audit trail date stamps the record for future reference. The system automatically creates a history record for every payroll transaction. With Payroll Accounting, you have the ability to tailor the system to your organization's requirements. When policy or legislative changes occur, you can adapt the system. Payroll Accounting provides numerous standard reports, as well as the capability to create reports that meet your organization's requirements.

Integration. HR Payroll Accounting maintains information on employees in a master file shared with all other HR components. The R/3 system writes payroll data into Controlling, Financial Accounting, and Logistics.

Global solutions. Whether your business operates only in one country or has expanded to international locations, SAP has the solution for all your payroll requirements. With country-specific versions of R/3 Payroll Accounting, you can fulfill language, currency, and regulatory requirements. At this time, SAP offers solutions for over twenty countries, including

Austria, Belgium, France, Great Britain, Germany, Japan, the Netherlands, Switzerland and the USA. SAP is constantly adding new country-specific solutions.

Time management. SAP R/3 HR Time Management is a powerful tool that helps you administer and evaluate data related to the time your employees spend working. This component can simplify your efforts whether your organization uses centralized or decentralized data to determine employee working hours.

Time data. R/3 HR Time Management manages work schedules efficiently and effectively by automating schedule generation and allowing flexible definition of time models and schedules for each location and organization level. With Time Management, you can set flexible working hours and process work notices as times are recorded. Individual and group piecework calculation for employee incentive wages is also available through the incentive wages feature.

Time evaluation. The Time Evaluation component allows daily processing of employee time data. It is a flexible tool designed to handle complicated evaluation rules to fulfill regulatory requirements and determine overtime and other time-related data. The Time Evaluation component stores your organizations' business rules and automatically validates hours worked and wage types. The results of time evaluation can be shown on a time sheet that provides a detailed overview of daily balances and time wage types.

Time management review. With R/3 HR Time Management, you have special transaction capabilities designed to support time clerks in their daily tasks. It provides all necessary information and tools to review and maintain employee time data. If for any reason the entered data is incorrect, an error handling feature makes the corrections.

Integration and interfaces. Time Management is integrated with Payroll Accounting, Controlling, Production Planning, Plant Maintenance, Project System, External Services, and Shift Planning. SAP also has standardized communication channels and protocols for many external data entry systems. R/3 Plant Data Collection (PDC) serves as an integration tool linking plant systems to all SAP business applications. As employee, machine, and work order data is received, PDC automatically assigns it to the appropriate system.

Reports and analyses. SAP R/3's Time Management component provides a variety of standard reports that assist in tracking and analyzing employee time with completeness and accuracy.

Shift planning. With the R/3 HR Shift Planning sub-component, you are able to arrange a target plan that can be drafted for any given period. You can plan your shifts according to requirements taking into consideration all criteria, including absences due to leave or sickness, and employee requests for time off. Shift Planning keeps you informed at all times of any staff excess or deficit; a convenient planning board is provided for guidance when entering and copying shifts for any designated period of time. Furthermore, you can check the plans at any time against rules governing employees' working time, for example, to detect non-compliance with relevant legislation.

All time data relating to your employees is centrally administered by R/3 HR Time Management. This means that not just the planned working time but also short-term changes to shift plan brought about by, for example, sickness or overtime are relayed directly to the Time Management component.

Another advantage of Shift Planning is that it enables you to temporarily assign an employee or employees to another organizational unit where they are needed, allowing for a temporary change of cost centre.

Shift Planning also allows you to view and print out your plans in MS-EXCEL at all times.

Qualifications and requirements. With HR qualifications, you can profile predefined tasks and prerequisites of each position in your organization. Further, you can profile the qualifications of employees and external candidates under consideration for each position. A comparison of the qualifications and profiles assists you in selecting individuals for further consideration.

Career and succession planning. Effective personnel development planning ensures that the goals of the organization and the goals of the employees are in harmony. The benefits of such planning include improvements in employee performance, employee potential, staff quality, working climate, and employee morale. R/3 HR Career and Succession Planning subcomponent provides organizations with a method of modelling suitable career opportunities for employees within the company.

Additional education and training programmes. R/3 Human Resources makes it possible to determine the areas in which employees need further training. Once this is established, you can then draw up individual plans for further education.

Training and event management. R/3 HR Training and Event Management component assists you with planning, managing, and analyzing your scheduled seminars, training courses, and business events. Detailed information for each of the events is maintained to facilitate production of event catalogues and schedules.

Training programmes and business events. This subcomponent includes tools to maintain information on the internal or external organizers of each event, as well as details such as prerequisites, objectives, content, time schedule, prices, capacity, locations, attendee billing information, and budgets. Resources such as instructors, rooms, equipment, and course materials can be automatically suggested, saving you a great deal of data entry time.

Registration and booking. With the help of data fast entry, you can book, rebook, and cancel attendees at very short notice. In doing so, the course prerequisites, as well as the availability of the attendees, are checked. The integrated functionality of Room Reservations Planning helps you choose a room on the basis of such factors as capacity, room design, and available facilities. On completion of a training course, appraisal forms can be automatically issued. Appraisals can be carried out for instructors, attendees, business events, and training courses. You can define the appraisal criteria for every appraisal type.

Charge determination and invoicing. Training and Event Management automatically determines the charge per attendee on the basis of the required resources. Attendee charges can be calculated internally via SAP R/3 Cost Accounting and invoiced externally using SAP R/3 Sales and Distribution.

Trends and highlights

Internet and intranet improve your internal and external communication.

SAP business workflow helps you distribute tasks automatically at the right time to the right employee.

Employee self-service serves up efficiency and savings.

Internet and intranet. Both the global Internet and company's Intranet are synonymous with easy data access and exchange. Thanks to user-friendly graphic web browsers and open standards, and protocols such as TCP/IP. The latest information is always available at your fingertips. The R/3 system is the first business application software that offers a special Internet functionality for a large number of business processes, such as personnel marketing.

The Internet gives you the opportunity to advertise vacancies in your company to a vast audience of potential applicants all over the world. The applicant is then able to make a general inquiry or be more selective, for example, specifying a preferred geographical region. The application itself could be carried out online by calling up an application form, filling it out and returning it by e-mail. The application would subsequently be processed automatically in R/3 HR. By sending applicants their own ID or password via e-mail, you can even give them the option of monitoring the progress of their application.

On a company-internal level, R/3 HR also makes searching for the right contact person easier; though till recently this has often not been the case, particularly in larger companies. Now, however, every employee can refer to an employee directory where the most important employee information, such as name, position, department, telephone number, and possibly even a photo, is stored. By using different search criteria, the relevant contact person can be found in no time at all.

SAP business workflow. The SAP R/3 Business Workflow component provides new impetus to work routines within HR. Because Business Workflow coordinates and monitors business processes step by step, activities processing is much more efficient. This means that all users automatically receive a list of their tasks in their R/3 Mail System inbox. Once the work is completed, R/3 Business Workflow starts the next predefined work step, and sends the relevant messages.

In HR Recruitment, for example, the following processes are automated:

> •Submission of application forms •Planning and holding of interviews •Drawing up contract offers •Preparing new appointments •Monitoring of rejected applications.

A range of workflow techniques, such as optical archiving, mailing, and office communication can be used at every stage. In addition to this, SAP has included other business processes in the R/3 Business Workflow component. It is also possible to portray new processes that are individually tailored to a particular business.

Employee self-service. HR Employee Self-Service components are user-friendly. This means that the HR department no longer has to perform such time-consuming and costly activities as issuing information and maintaining data. The HR staff can now concentrate their efforts on corporate areas of greater strategic value. The Employee Self-Service components also increase the quality of information in the organization.

Other functions available in this package are:

Address and dependents data. Employees can check, supplement, and even change their address data. They can enter data on new family members, or change existing information on next of kin.

Leave entitlement and requests. Employees can check their current leave entitlement and submit leave requests. Using SAP R/3 Business Workflow, the latter can be forwarded directly to the person responsible for authorizing leave.

Benefits data. Employees can see their benefits data online.

Travel expense recording and data. Employees can enter expense account data online using an Excel format. All company regulations on flat rates, per diems, meals, accommodations and so forth are taken into consideration. Employees can also check the processing status of any expense account data they may have entered in the system.

Certificates of employment. Employees can call up certificates of employment, which they can then submit to banks, for example.

SAP's customary authorization and data security measures also apply to employee self-service components. Employees can only access their own data and require a user ID specified by the system and a personal password to do so.

One can determine whether the employees can change their personal data or are authorized to view only their own data. Furthermore, changed data can be sent to the human resources department for checking and confirmation.

Example of an Indian ERP Package

During the 1990s, many Indian software companies developed ERP packages which were sold and implemented at hundreds of companies across India. Some of these packages have even been successfully implemented overseas. Sara ERP is one such package from Mumbai based Sara Infotech. The company was established to create software products that would compete globally in terms of quality, functionality and cost. Today, this company has developed over a dozen packages, including its flagship package **Sara Intelligent Enterprise Management System (Sara IEMS).**

Sara IEMS is a comprehensive ERP III package, comprising ERP, CRM, SCM, Business Intelligence and Interface with various equipment and instruments, all in one single application and one database. The system is suitable for Discrete as well as Process manufacturing industries. The system also has seamless integration with DCS, SCADA and various equipment, instruments and meters. Sara is also developing its own DCS and SCADA systems as part of its IEMS. Sara IEMS is fully modular and, if needed, only a few modules can be implemented as per the requirement of the client. Other modules can be implemented at a later date and integrated with the existing modules. Sara IEMS is priced module-wise, enabling a client to start with a few modules and a lower investment. Sara IEMS modules can also be integrated with other Enterprise applications such as SAP, BAAN, J D Edwards, Siebel, and PeopleSoft.

It is observed that most of the basic functionality required by clients is available in almost all the ERP packages. But users are unhappy because the ERPs have not been implemented properly and the organizations have not derived the expected benefits even after spending millions of dollars. In order to facilitate better customization and implementation, Sara sends at least one member of its development team along with its marketing partners. It mainly works through its marketing partners in India, Thailand, Malaysia, Singapore, Australia and other countries.

Sara started developing its ERP package in 1995 and it was ready by 1999—an effort of approximately 300 man-years. Later it developed CRM, Business Intelligence, Interface with DCS, SCADA and other equipment, instruments, meters, etc. Sara has also enhanced its ERP package for certain verticals like hospitals, hotels, insurance, etc. to take into account their front-office functions. Sara ERP has been successfully implemented in diverse companies in India, Thailand, Indonesia, Malaysia, and other countries.

THE ARRIVAL OF ERP III

In the 1980s, ERP packages consisted primarily of business functions covering Purchase, Sales, Finance, Manufacturing, Quality Control, Plant Maintenance, etc. All these were integrated into one application. Later on, in the 90s, customers/suppliers database and queries were incorporated into ERP packages through the Web, and it was named as EERP (Extended ERP). During 1992-1995, some companies like Siebel and Clarify developed CRM packages and provided interface with leading ERP packages. By 2000, most ERP vendors had incorporated CRM into their ERP/Business applications. These packages which have integrated ERP, Web and CRM, are termed as *ERP II packages*.

During 1995–98, some software vendors like COGNOS and Brio developed Business Intelligence packages which provide interface with the leading ERP packages. We expect that by 2003, most of the leading ERP vendors will also incorporate Business Intelligence, Auditor Information System and Transfer Pricing as standard modules in their products, and such an integrated package should be called *ERP III*. Figure 6.1 represents the ERP III Architecture in its integrated form.

In many manufacturing companies, most of the modules of ERP packages are implemented, but the production module is not implemented properly because it requires too much of manual data entry for the readings of various equipment instruments like DCS, SCADA for attributes such as energy, temperature, pressure, humidity, weight, and attendance. Most companies have separate stand-alone system to handle such equipment.

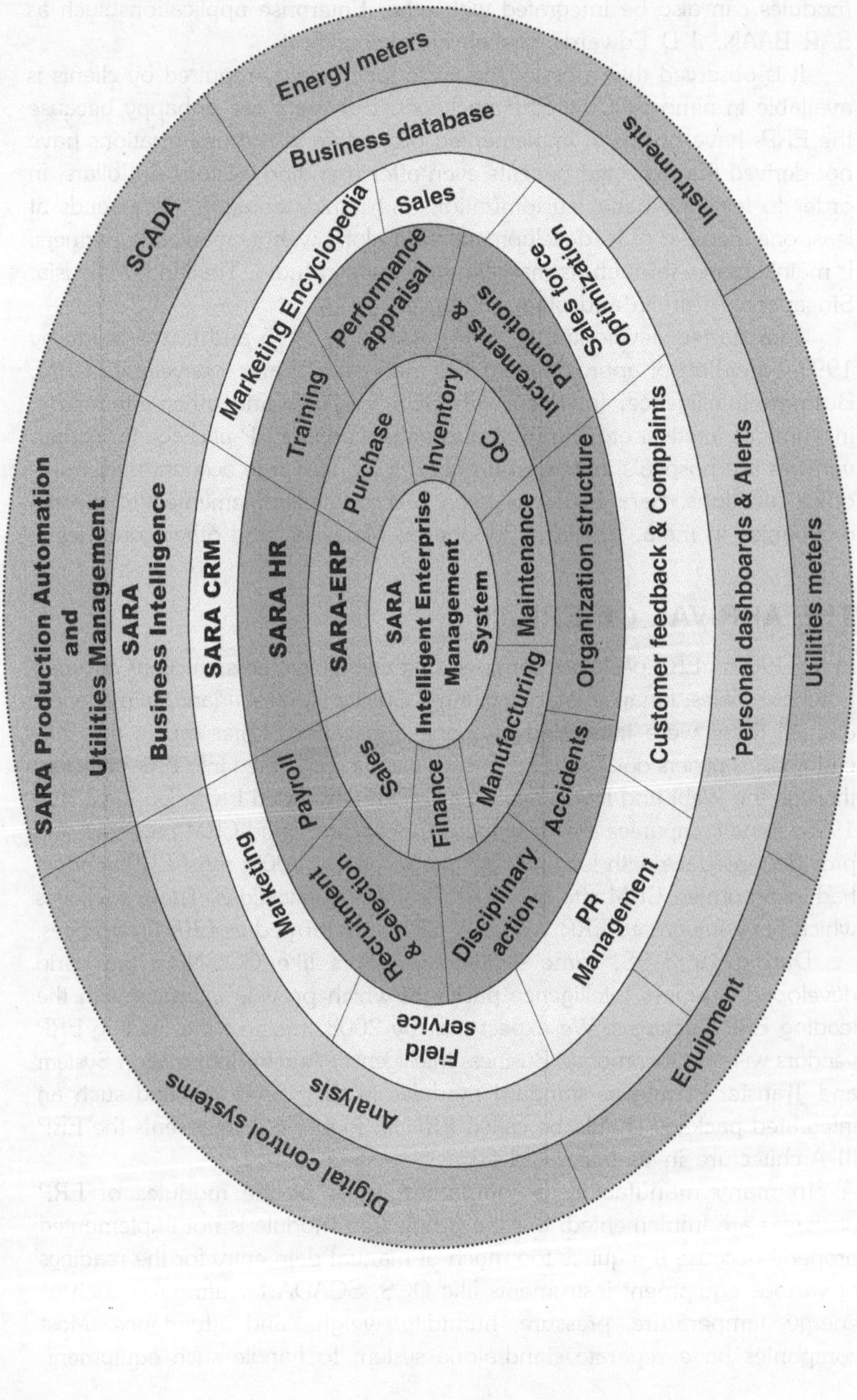

Fig. 6.1 SARA ERP III architecture.

Ideally, all these reading instruments should go directly into the ERP database. Such an integrated system should be rightly called **Intelligent Enterprise Management System (IEMS)**. Some of the vendors like Sara have already incorporated Business Intelligence and interface with Equipment/ Instruments in their ERP, and many other vendors are likely to incorporate these modules into their products in the coming years.

Sara IEMS has the following subsystems:

- Sara-ERP
- Sara HR
- Sara CRM
- Sara Business Intelligence
- Sara Plant and Machinery Interface

Sara ERP Subsystem has the following modules:

- Sales forecasting and business planning
- Purchase management
- Subcontracting
- Inventory control
- Accounts receivable
- Accounts payable
- General ledger
- Master production scheduling
- Capacity requirement planning
- Material requirement planning
- Shopfloor controls and work-in-process
- Production management
- Scrap accounting and control
- Quality control
- Sales order processing
- Invoicing and dispatching
- Customer complaints
- Laboratory tests and results
- Payroll
- Fixed assets management
- After sales service
- Distribution resource planning
- Human resource development
- Plant maintenance
- Budgeting and costing

- Fixed deposit accounting
- Project management
- Excise, Sales tax, VAT, TDS accounting

Sara HR Subsystem has the following modules:

- Organisation structure
- Manpower planning
- Recruitment and selection
- Performance appraisal
- Increments and promotions
- Training
- Deputation/Tour
- Perks not a part of payroll
- Disciplinary actions
- Accidents
- Separation

Sara CRM Subsystem has the following modules:

- Marketing management
- Marketing encyclopedia
- Sales management
- Customer feedback and complaints
- Salesforce optimisation
- Field service
- Partner relationship management
- Opinion leaders management
- PR management
- Employee relationship management
- Customer training
- Customer surveys and their analysis

Sara Business Intelligence has the following modules:

- Analysis
- Personal dash boards and alerts
- Interface with business databases

Sara Plant and Machinery Interface provides seamless interface with DCS, SCADA and other equipments, instruments and meters.

PROBLEMS

6.1 Draw a matrix showing functionality provided by the various prominent (at least three) ERP packages.

6.2 Rank the various ERP packages in the order of their Market Share. In your opinion, is "ERP domain shrinking or expanding"? Give reason for your answer. Is the same comment true for various individual packages as well?

6.3 Having been entrusted with the responsibility of convincing your senior management about going for an ERP solution, make a presentation covering various aspects such as the present trend, benefits of an ERP system over any legacy system, the risks involved, and scope of outsourcing support.

7

Marketing of ERP

An Overview

A study of the dynamics of the ERP market, how they evolve through a number of stages, and the characteristics of competitive behaviour, provides a basis for assessing market attractiveness and assists the ERP marketing personnel to choose the market, the market segment and to position themselves competitively. Underpinning this decision also lies a number of capability considerations. What is the organizations current competitive position? Is it a market leader or a challenger? Is it seeking a strong or dominant industry position or merely seeking to win a small but profitable sector of the industry. Does the stage of market maturation strongly suggest or preclude certain competitive initiatives? How does one position ERP? This chapter discusses the various strategies for positioning ERP in the market and the entire process of selling.

MARKET DYNAMICS AND COMPETITIVE STRATEGY

Studying the dynamics of the ERP market, how they evolve through a number of stages and the characteristics of competitive behaviour; provides a basis for assessing market attractiveness and assists the ERP marketing personnel in their choice of market, market segment and competitive positioning. Underpinning this decision also lie a number of capability considerations. What is the organization's and the ERP's current competitive position? Is it a market leader or is it a challenger? Is it seeking a strong or dominant industry position or is it merely seeking to win a small but profitable industry sector. Does the stage of market maturation strongly suggest or preclude certain competitive initiatives? How does one position ERP?

Managing the ERP Marketing Strategy Process

The competent marketing manager should have a deep understanding of the market and the product and know all about the process of managing marketing strategy from the organization's point of view. Marketing activity of ERP, no matter how enthusiastically pursued, is unlikely to be of much use unless it is set in a strategic context. The marketing manager's foremost job is to manage the marketing strategy process. This primarily means making the correct choice of markets and industry segments.

From industry choice to positioning. The choice is a complex endeavour. The manager must select at a broad generic level between the following strategies:

- Positioning the ERP and the implementation or service to meet the specialized needs of one segment,
- Positioning add-on products and services also to meet the needs of several separate segments, or
- Positioning the ERP to provide general appeal across many segments.

The choice of a target market results in a clear identification of the target group with which the organization wishes to develop a market relationship. The segmentation analysis leading to this decision yields an essential profile of target customers in terms of their buying needs and relevant individual or organizational characteristics.

When the target customer group has been chosen, the managerial challenge becomes that of positioning the company and its ERP or services relative to the preferences and acceptability of the target group and relative to existing and anticipated competitive offerings. The objective is to serve the customer and to outperform competitors by focusing the company's competencies in an appropriate manner.

Analysis for competitive positioning. To make a competitive positioning decision the manager must first know

1. customer purchase criteria,
2. customer preference concerning service or product performance on each criterion, and
3. customer perceptions of competing vendor and their products on each criterion.

Customer purchase criteria. The importance of understanding the criteria used in evaluating the alternative ERPs and services is stressed, not only because of their central role in explaining customer's favouring an ERP, but also because an appreciation of the nature and use of these criteria is fundamental to the positioning decision. Evaluative criteria are usually best conceived of as benefits sought by customers from competing products or services. The identification of such criteria which customers will use in making their evaluations not only allows us to understand their decision-making but also makes it possible to segment the market in terms of customers requiring a suitable ERP-based solution. Normally, there are several important purchase criteria involved in the buying pattern. In general, these may be categorized as:

- Price-related criteria (e.g. purchase price, discounts, multisite license price)
- Performance-related (i.e. functional) criteria (e.g. scalability, upgradability, user-friendliness, service and support facilities)
- Psychosocial criteria (e.g. acceptability to others, reputability and dependability of vendor)
- Quality
- Delivery schedule
- Multisite discounts offered
- Warranty provided
- After-sales service
- Credit terms
- Implementation strengths.

It becomes clear that, for an ERP to sell, it should come with a bundle of benefits a prospect should appreciate; and the perception of the ERP to enable the user to reap benefits lies at the heart of the customer's evaluation process.

Understanding the customer. The first step in formulating a positioning approach is to complete a basic listing of the criteria important to the target customers through formal research or, at the least, through personal questioning of buyers and reflection on experience in marketing to them successfully.

Some prospects will require the ERP sales people to give them the confidence that they understand their needs. It is very important for the ERP salesperson to take control of the discussions because the customer will ultimately never gain confidence, if he is allowed to ramble about his specific application, technology and environment without any initiative from the vendor.

Customer preferences. After the criteria have been identified, the next step is to identify customer preferences concerning ERP performance on each criterion. A map of customer preference is of enormous importance, as it documents explicitly an ideal service from the customer's viewpoint. In doing so, it provides one of the essential benchmarks relative to which an ERP and related service offering may then be positioned.

Customer perceptions of competing products. The next step that must be taken before making a positioning decision is to detail the perceived position of each competing product on each criterion. Significant marketing implications of the analysis now begin to appear. How the different ERPs differ is readily visible as is their ability (or inability) to match customer preferences.

The competitive positioning decision. Armed with such information the marketing team then decides how to position its ERP offering in the market. The position chosen is of a relative nature. It makes marketing sense insofar as it is chosen relative to the identified customer preferences and competitor performance on each important criterion and relative to the company's capabilities.

Promotion. The first step is to understand the difference between image and identity. People often form perceptions based on feedback from other organizations. It becomes very necessary before launching any promotion, to establish the identity of the ERP. Identity is based on characteristics that make an ERP what it is and what it is intended to provide. Once the identity is established, it is time to decide the **unique selling proposition (USP)**. The marketing concept rests on four pillars: target market, customer needs, integrated marketing, and profitability.

As for any product, the fundamental selling concept for an ERP takes an inside-out perspective. It starts with organization, focuses on the company's existing strengths, and calls for heavy selling and promoting to produce sales. The marketing concept takes an outside-in perspective. It starts with a well-defined market focused on customer needs, integrates all the activities that will affect customers, and produces sales by satisfying those needs.

Target market. Understanding the advantages and the limitations of the ERP, the company should target those prospects that will possibly look at what it is offering. Those companies do best which define their target market(s) carefully and prepare a tailored marketing programme.

Customer needs. A company can define its target market but fail to fully understand customer needs. Consider the following example. A customer says he wants an "inexpensive" car. The marketer must probe further. We can distinguish among five types of needs.

1. Stated needs (the customer wants an expensive car)
2. Real needs (the customer wants a car of which the operating cost, not the initial price, is low)
3. Unstated needs (the customer expects good service from the vendor)
4. Delight needs (the customer buys a car which would earn him complements)
5. Secret needs (the customer wants to be seen by friends as a value-oriented savvy consumer).

Responding only to the customer's stated need may not meet his expectations. Customer-oriented thinking requires the company to define customer needs from the customer's point of view. Every buying decision involves tradeoffs, and management cannot know what these are without researching the customers. Thus, a car buyer would like a safe, attractive, reliable, high-performance car that costs less than $10,000. Since all these features cannot be combined in one car, the car designer must take hard choices based on knowledge of customer tradeoffs.

In general, a company can respond to customers' requests by giving them what they want, or what they need, or what they really need. The key to professional marketing is to understand the customers' real needs and meet them more effectively than any competitor can.

Relationship Marketing—The Key

To understand customer relationship marketing, we must first examine the process involved in attracting and keeping customers. The starting point is, suspect everyone who might conceivably buy your ERP and implementation service. The company looks hard at the suspects to determine who the most likely prospects may be, the people who have a strong potential interest in the product and the ability to pay for it. Disqualified prospects are those whom the company rejects because they have poor credit or would be unprofitable. The company hopes to convert many of its qualified prospects into first-time customers and to then convert those satisfied first-time customers into repeat customers. Both first-time and repeat customers may continue to buy from competitors as well. The company then acts to convert repeat product categories. The next challenge is to turn clients into advocates, customers who praise the company and encourage others to buy from it. The ultimate challenge is to turn advocates into partners, where the customer and the company actively work together. At the same time, it must be recognized that some customers will inevitably become inactive or drop out, for reasons of bankruptcy, moves to other locations, dissatisfaction, and so on. The company's challenge is to react to dissatisfied customers through customer win-back strategies. It is often easier to retract ex-customers than to find new ones especially when they are dissatisfied with the existing solution.

The belief is at the core of the new view of business processes, which places marketing at the beginning of the business planning process. Instead of emphasizing, making and selling, companies that take this view of the business process see themselves as part of the value creation and delivery sequence. This sequence consists of three parts.

The first phase, choosing the value, represents the "homework" that the marketing personnel must do before actually positioning the ERP in the market. The marketing staff must segment the market, select the appropriate market target, and develop the offered plan's value positioning. The formula **segmentation, targeting, positioning (STP)** is the essence of strategic marketing.

Once the business unit has chosen the value, it is ready to provide it. The ERP's specifications and services must be detailed, a target price established, and the product made and distributed. Developing specific product features, prices, and distribution occur at this stage and are parts of tactical marketing—the second phase of the value creation and delivery sequence.

The task in the third phase entails communicating the value. Here, further tactical marketing occurs in utilizing the sales force, sales promotion, advertising, and other promotional tasks to inform the market about the product. The marketing process consists of analyzing opportunities, developing marketing strategies, planning marketing programmes, and managing the marketing effort.

Developing Marketing Strategies

Should the organization offer the ERP at a premium price with excellent service that is well-advertised and aimed at higher-end markets? Or should it aim for a product to be offered at a medium price with limited functionality?

After launch, the ERP positioning strategy will have to be modified at different stages in the product life cycle: introduction, growth, maturity, and decline. Furthermore, the strategy choice will depend on whether the organization plays the role of market leader, challenger or follower. Finally, strategy will have to take into account changing global opportunities and challenges.

Planning Marketing Programmes

To transform marketing strategy into marketing programmes, marketing managers must take basic decisions on marketing expenditures, marketing mix, and marketing allocation. First, the organization must decide the level of their marketing expenditures in their marketing budget as a percentage of the sales goal. A particular company may spend more than the normal percentage ratio in the hope of achieving a higher market share. Second, the company also has to decide how to divide the total marketing budget among the various tools in the marketing mix.

Finally, marketers must decide on the allocation of the marketing budget to the ERP, channels, promotion media, and sales areas—direct versus distributor sales, direct mail advertising versus trade-magazine advertising or any support service that can provide a competitive advantage in the competitive marketplace.

A critical marketing mix tool includes the various activities, the company undertakes to make the product accessible and available to target customers. It must identify, recruit, and link various marketing synergies with the management consultants to help recommend the ERP and services efficiently to the target corporate.

Promotion, the fourth marketing mix tool, includes all the activities the company undertakes to communicate and promote its products in the target market. The organization has to hire, train, and motivate salespeople. It has to set up communication and promotion programmes consisting of advertising, sales promotions, public relations, and direct and on-line marketing.

Marketing Strategy

The product manager now outlines the broad marketing strategy or "game plan" that he or she will use to accomplish the plan's objectives. The marketing strategy is often presented in list form:

- Target market: To identify industry sectors
- Positioning: Define and emphasize USP of the product
- Product line: Add-on products
- Price: Competitive price
- Distribution: Synergy with hardware/software vendors
- Sales force: To expand by 10% and introduce a national account-management system
- Service: To provide widely available and quick service by competent professionals
- Advertising: To develop a new advertising campaign that supports the positioning
- Seminars/ Trade shows: To participate in trade shows and seminars

- Strategy: To emphasize USP in the advertisements and commercials; increase the advertising budget by 20%.

Action Programmes

The marketing plan must specify the broad marketing programmes designed to achieve the business objectives. Each marketing strategy element must now be elaborated to answer the questions: What will be done? When will it be done? Who will do it? How much will it cost?

Marketing and environmental stimuli enter the buyer's consciousness. The buyer's characteristics and decision processes lead to certain purchase decisions. The marketer's task is to understand what happens in the buyer's consciousness between arrival or outside stimuli; and his purchase decisions. They must answer two questions:

How do the buyers characteristics—cultural, social and psychological—influence buying behaviour? How does the buyer make purchasing decisions?

Participants in the ERP Buying Process

Who participates in the buying of the ERP and the services worth millions? The buying centre is any part of the organization that plays any of the following roles in the purchase decision.

- Those who request that some ERP must be purchased. They may be users who initiate the proposal and help define the ERP requirements.
- Those who will use the software or service. In many cases, the users define the specifications and also provide information for evaluating alternatives.
- Technical personnel.
- People who decide on ERP requirements and/or on vendors.
- People who authorize the proposed actions of deciders or buyers.
- People who have formal authority to select the vendor and arrange the purchase terms.
- Buyers may help shape product specifications, but they play their major role in selecting vendors and negotiating. In more complex purchases, the buyers might include high-level managers participating in the negotiations.

Within any organization, the buying centre will vary in the number and type for different classes of products. According to a Pentagon research survey, the average number of people involved in a buying decision ranges between three and four. There is a trend toward team-based buying. Another Pentagon survey found that 87% of purchasing executives at Fortune 1000 companies expect teams of people from departments and functions to be making buying decisions in the year to target their efforts properly, business marketers have to figure out who the major decision participants are. What decisions do they influence? What is their area of influence? What evaluation criteria do they use?

Who will Require ERP?

Before the start of any ERP selling process, the salesperson should find out the suitability of his or her ERP for a particular organization and should accept the fact that ERP will be certainly required by

- Organizations with a vision for leadership. To be a leader, it is necessary that the organizations make the best use of the available resources.
- Organizations that are customer-service driven.
- Organizations that are under tremendous pressure to be competitive because of fierce competition and are expected to perform above their level to sustain their position in the market place.
- Organizations that enter an already crowded market.
- An organization in which the business processes are too complex and which, therefore, requires the highest level of coordination among its employees. To achieve this, they require data from all departments that are integrated for correct decision-making and analysis.

The Actual Sales Cycle

Based on the needs of the organization and understanding of the criteria that the customer will look at before buying an ERP system, as shown in Figure 7.1 the sales personnel should diligently follow the steps described below to ensure that the ERP product represented by their organization is considered.

Step 1: Prospecting. This exercise should be undertaken to generate a pipeline of prospects to assess the ERP automation needs of the organization. The pipeline should include the top 500 companies, companies which are willing to embrace the latest in technology and have the approved budget. Many of the companies seek the help of management consultants like the Big 6 to identify the right ERP solution for their enterprise. Hence, it is important that the ERP vendor develop a relationship with these firms, so that they may ultimately recommend their ERP.

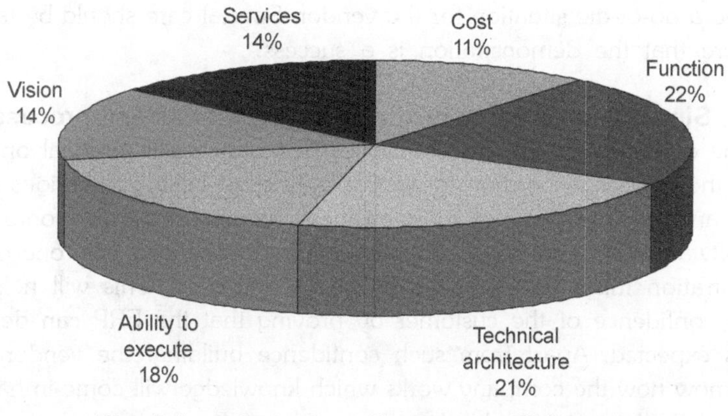

Fig. 7.1 Criteria for selecting an ERP system.

Step 2: Qualification of prospect. This is one of the important aspects of the entire selling process as identification and assessment of the seriousness of the prospect are carried out and understood at this point. If proper qualification is not done, then the salesperson may end up wasting his/her time talking to the wrong prospect. The qualification also becomes important, as this is the list of prospects to whom a possible sale can be accomplished.

Step 3: Corporate marketing presentation. The first step towards proving your strength either in terms of the organization or in terms of the ERP product is through a "jazzy" corporate presentation. This presentation should cover details about the company, its corporate mission, philosophy, culture, available infrastructure and the list of customer organizations in which implementation has been successfully carried out. On the product side, the important features and functionalities, tools available for customization, the service and support available, upgrade policies, implementation support and so on should be stated and specifically how the ERP under consideration can help the user to achieve a competitive edge in manufacturing methods and selling processes. Ultimately, an ERP is implemented for the organization to become or remain competitive and it is very important that the presentation expressly communicates to the senior management, the tangible and the intangible benefits of implementing an ERP.

Step 4: Demonstration of the key features of the software. This is the most crucial process in the entire sales cycle as most of the decision-makers and user groups will participate in this demonstration. Its success is directly related to the ability of the sales/technical staff to effectively relate and map the business processes of the organization to the features available on the ERP software. This requires the technical consultants to understand the various business processes of an organization. This process could be a do-or-die situation for the vendor. Special care should be taken to ensure that the demonstration is a success.

Step 5: Simulation of some of the company's business processes. After the demonstration is successfully carried out, it will be ideal on the part of the vendor to be more proactive by way of talking to various user groups and getting some of their business processes mapped onto the ERP software. This process of simulation should be followed by one more demonstration this time on the ERP being simulated. This will help in gaining confidence of the customer by proving that the ERP can deliver what is expected. Apart from such confidence building, the vendor will get to know how the company works which knowledge will come in handy for actual implementation, in case the vendor manages to close the sale of the ERP.

Step 6: Closing the sale. This is ultimate and most tricky step in the entire sales cycle. If the above-mentioned steps are successfully carried out, 80% of the selling is done. The final 20% depends on the price, the discounts offered, the track record of the organization in successful implementation of the ERP, and of course, on the impressive client list.

Finally, the most natural choice will be an ERP which provides scalable architecture making it possible for all enterprises to cost-effectively implement the software. The software should have a client/server architecture, should run on most popular environments and be Internet enabled to provide customers with the operational flexibility they need to be the leaders in their chosen market. And above all, it must instill confidence in the mind of the prospective buyer that the solution they are deciding on is the right fit for their type of business and the service provider will take them through the pre- and post-implementation stages of the software.

PROBLEMS

7.1 Discuss the prevalent situation in terms of marketing of an ERP solution. Your answer should cover the following:

(1) Product marketing

(2) Solution marketing

(3) ERP implementation services marketing

(4) Any other related issues such as the role of management consultancy firms in the marketing of ERP.

7.2 Draw a diagram to describe ERP marketing process including ERP sales cycle.

7.3 Present a case to convince a prospective customer about the suitability of your ERP product in his business environment.

8

Case Studies

An Overview

This chapter presents a few case studies on some of the major companies that have implemented ERP solutions worldwide and how they have benefited from this implementation.

In the past few years, ever since the ERP concept was accepted by industry, various companies have embraced one ERP vendor or another. These industries range from automobiles to pharmaceuticals, and banks to distribution and insurance companies. However, at present, the manufacturing and the distribution industries head the list of ERP customers. These companies have gone for a variety of ERP packages on different platforms. One thing that comes out clearly is that all these companies have benefited substantially in improving their competitive abilities. It also comes out that, selecting an ERP has been a strategic rather than a tactical decision which has stemmed, from a top-down thinking. In this chapter, we have tried to present a scenario of wide-ranging ERP implementations compiled from various published materials. We hope this will help readers to put the entire ERP practice in its true perspective. It also brings out the various issues involved in ERP selection, implementation and post-implementation. These case studies also throw light on why one should decide on going the ERP way.

MERCEDES-BENZ

Known worldwide for producing automobiles of the highest quality, Mercedes-Benz uses Baan software at its engine remanufacturing factory in Berlin. With more than 650 engine variations, the requirements for manufacturing applications software were quite complex. They primarily opted for Baan's software as they realized that Baan fulfilled the specific demands of engine reconditioning without customization as it provides for flexible customization capabilities.

Mercedes-Benz is one of the leading suppliers of automobiles in the world. The product range includes a large variety of vehicles from exclusive cars to universal commercial vehicles. Within Mercedes-Benz Inc., some production sites hold the position of suppliers in order to achieve an efficient division of labour. One of these sites is the engine factory in Berlin (2600 employees), which produces complete engines as well as engine parts. One department of this factory is in charge of the reconditioning of old engines (approx. 450 employees).

Since the engine is not only the heart of the automobile but also a very cost-intensive component, the reconditioning of usable parts is especially important from the ecological and economical points of view. The reconditioning in terms of dismantling, identification, chemistry and reconditioning of individual parts is quite similar to the operations in a workshop, but when it comes to the assembling of engines, it is more like small-lot production.

In 1993, the engine parts reconditioning department of the production site in Berlin had to decide whether an individual or a standard software solution should be used to achieve more economical manufacture of rebuilt engines. Long machining time, low transparency of the manufacturing process, absence of uniform information about bills of materials and, to a large extent, manual calculation of requirements were the most significant weaknesses of the former manufacturing procedure. These weaknesses were identified through a profound analysis of the actual procedure. In the development of the target procedure, optimum PPS procedures were taken as the guideline. Workshops were organized with the PPS suppliers, during which the PPS system was chosen in accordance with the target business. Step by step, TRITON appeared to be the best suited PPS system. TRITON was chosen because it is very flexible and can, therefore, handle the multiple requirements of the manufacturing of rebuilt engines (variants and alternative parts issues).

The modified TRITON 2.2 on a HP9000 system. The operational system is installed on HP 9000/h50 with a 448 MB main memory and 2 × 9 GB mirrored disks. The standby system on a HP 9000/i50 with a 448 MB main memory is linked to the operational computer by a switch-over concept and is used as a development computer. Sixty PCs, 36 terminals, 15 Alpha terminals and 15 laser printers are available for the users.

After only six months of using TRITON, all item masters and the 6500 construction kits of 850 engine variants were registered. Then the routings were defined and drastically reduced (by 85%) due to the definition of parts families. In May 1994, required quantities started to be calculated by means of an extended MRP, and in Autumn 1994 the production order control started. Since January 1995, the system is in operation and completed by the addition of the inventory control and machine-aided disposition. The costing control is to be added in the future.

It was observed that after only a few weeks of operation, the former standard situation of incorrectly issued parts became less tense. The milestone reports have led to transparency of the manufacturing process, which again facilitates early recognition of problematic parts and an early adoption of accelerating measures. The transfer from a pure manual disposition to a machine-controlled disposition was the most difficult task. The extended MRP calculates the required quantities on its own by using the complex structures of the bills of materials with their multiple possibilities of alternative parts. The required quantities are then used by the planners to issue the corresponding manufacturing orders or purchase orders. The tests of these customized functions were more complex than anticipated. During operation there were some problems resulting from the always new constellations in the complex algorithms, but in the meantime, they gained control of most of the problems.

Management and IT people at Benz were convinced that choosing TRITON standard software plus adaptations was the right decision. The costs involved in individual programming would have been much higher and they would have integrated some of the old concepts into the software which they have now avoided by means of very good organization. All in all, it can be stated that as a result of using TRITON and the accompanying organi-zational procedures, their business operations were simplified and made more secure and transparent. The employees now have a better view of the whole process chain and the targeted rationalization goal was surpassed.

KEE HIN INDUSTRIES

Kee Hin Industries (KHIND) specializes in electrical products and is extremely innovative and versatile. The company is well known for its ability to manufacture a wide variety of electrical products which range from sophisticated electrical home appliances to basic wiring accessories.

KHIND was started in the early 1960s when its first product was a simple electrical outlet. The company has carved out a competitive niche for itself in the electronics industry where hundreds of different electrical products are produced. KHIND has an extensive product range which consists of table and decorative lamps, home appliances including fans in assorted colours and sizes; wire extension rollers and trailing sockets, and electrical and wiring accessories. KHIND is a market leader for table lamps, cable clips, electric fans, sensor lights, magnetic starts, money detectors, extension rollers and trailing sockets both in Malaysia and in Singapore. The company also has the distinction of being the licensee of Disney lamps as well as distributor for several other manufacturers' products.

The company has done itself proud with its manufacturing flexibility and also its extensive distribution network across Malaysia and Singapore. Manufacturing is done both for the domestic and overseas markets. Kee Hin exports its products to more than twenty countries in Europe, South East Asia, the Middle East, Africa, South America and the USA.

KHIND products are marketed by its marketing arm, KHIND Marketing Sdn Bhd in Malaysia. The marketing company has several offices located across Malaysia. KHIND products are easily and quickly available because each KHIND Marketing office is equipped with its own warehouse and dispatch vehicles to ensure fast delivery.

Kee Hin Industries realized that to hold on to its competitive edge, it needs to focus on maintaining its high-quality standards, keep its pricing competitive and increase responsiveness to customer needs. Kee Hin wanted to be more efficient in handling the sales process, offer better control over the manufacturing, and to improve insight into its inventory.

In 1995, KHIND chose Baan's TRITON for its manufacturing plants as well as for implementation in KHIND Marketing for handling the distribution functions.

Before adopting TRITON, KHIND was using a manual system. All items were entered manually and many times needed to be re-entered when transferred from KHIND Marketing to the KHIND Manufacturing plant. This process was time-consuming and error-prone. This company also has a wide product range offering over 300 different products and has over 900 different products if its different brand names and colours are taken into account. To manually keep track of the product range required tremendous effort. Keeping their specific requirements in view, in 1993, KHIND realized the importance and the benefit that could be achieved from an integrated information system.

The search for a new IT solution was started in November 1993. The company set up a steering committee spearheaded by their Assistant General Manager and started looking for MRP II software suppliers. Once the budget was determined and the project approved, it started moving. The information systems staff was trained by an outside consultant on MRP II concepts. This process was considered important as they had used a manual system and needed to understand the concepts and benefits of an MRP II system in order to implement it.

Demonstrations of the software vendors were seen and a short list was created. The evaluation criteria included profiles of the software principle and the software vendor. Another important factor was the time it would take to implement the solution. This was treated as critical. In their visits to MRP sites earlier on in the evaluation of the software, KHIND personnel had noticed that some systems were taking one to two years to implement and felt it was critical that the project become operational as fast as possible so that they could then optimize the system. KHIND considered the implementation process so important that they even spent time in the evaluation process on meeting the people who would implement the software.

The software's function and features were evaluated along with the project costs. The future upgrade path of the software and the scalability were thoroughly examined. In December 1995, the decision was made to acquire Baan's software KHIND selected Baan software as it offered a solution for planning and controlling KHIND's activities within the company. KHIND found that the TRITON solution could dramatically help their company retain its leadership position. TRITON provided the integration between KHIND manufacturing and KHIND Marketing that would benefit both companies. The integrated company-wide information system would increase productivity and improve customer service.

Another significant advantage of TRITON was the multi-language features of the software and the trainers of Baan Malaysia. "Baan Malaysia provided training in several languages including English, Malay, Hawkin and Chinese which was a necessary precondition for Kee Hin. The company purchased TRITON Manufacturing, TRITON Distribution, TRITON Finance and TRITON Tools and installed the system on IBM hardware. The database selected was Baan's own TRITON Base. The implementation had one goal, it was clear that they needed to have the system operational as soon as possible to keep their employees motivated and to benefit from the system. Implementation is being done in cooperation with Baan Malaysia. The implementation project was named Excellent Work. The progress of the project was communicated by means of banners in all depart-ments involved, indicating the target dates for all to see. It was considered important that progress of the project be communicated internally so that it would get the employees excited. A bulletin board was also used which had the status of the project listed and the priorities.

With the TRITON system implementation, Kee Hin expected to see the benefits of efficiency. With orders being keyed in and accessed by the manufacturing plant, the cycle would become less cumbersome and able to react more quickly to customer requests. The TRITON system also enables order entry personnel to check stock levels online and again improve customer service.

The TRITON system would also allow KHIND to reduce inventory by enabling managers to track inventory, analyze costs and improve stock control. They would then be able to have better control over their manufacturing and distribution processes. This would, in turn, contribute to increasing productivity and also improve the responsiveness to customers' requirements. In addition, they would be able to evaluate all the costs associated with their products.

BULL ELECTRONICS ANGERS PLANT MANUFACTURERS

The Bull Anger plant in the Loire Valley, France, employs almost 1400 people. The company's activities are the manufacture of printed circuit boards, assembly of computer systems and the distribution of products throughout Europe. Bull's production is for both Bull and OEM manufacturers worldwide. The plant originally started production of the dps 7000 and dps 8000 mainframe systems, but Anger also receives more orders from third party constructors.

Angers has a complicated production environment. The computer systems are all configured to fit the requirements of the customer. The number of variants for a customer system is extremely large, for example, the size of the computer, the processing power and the additional features can all vary. The computer systems are, therefore, produced in a **make-to-order environment**, while the printed circuit boards (PCB) are manufactured in a **series** or **repetitive batch-production environment**.

The Bull plant is part of Group Bull which is a leader in the worldwide information technology industry. The company is focused on satisfying customer demands for information systems solutions to business problems and challenges. For Bull Angers, this translates into producing better, faster, cheaper computers for their customers.

Before the implementation of TRITON, IT system the Bull Angers factories' had four separate applications for logistics, purchasing, and manufacturing. The system was based on mainframe proprietary software, was not integrated, and information was not accessible by every department. The four separate systems being extremely old entailed high maintenance costs and were not flexible to adapt to the growing needs of the company. The old system was found to be too rigid and inflexible to attend efficiently to users' requests and the company started looking for a more flexible system and a fully integrated solution that could fit the production environment obtaining within the company. Their old system was unmanageable and took several days to interface between the different systems and this was causing delays in their order processing flow. In short, the systems had become too slow to react and were difficult and expensive to maintain. So, in 1993 the company set up a project to define future development based on standard software and a new technical architecture.

Changes in the way the factory operated, both in terms of its manufacturing methods and its production systems, had become not just strategically desirable but absolutely vital for survival. Their production processes had to be brought in line with the reaction times demanded by the market. They found that a turnaround time of less than 24 hours for an order is essential and the market is no longer prepared to accept a delivery time of several days. Several MRP solutions were evaluated and a final short list was drawn up.

One of the main reasons for selecting TRITON was that the software had been fully integrated. The company was looking for a single system to replace the separate systems. TRITON was found to be integrable with other software for shop floor control and engineering change control to allow for seamless information exchange. TRITON provided an integrated and flexible system that could streamline the business processes and offered the ability to change whenever the company changed.

TRITON was also able to fit the production environment found in the Bull plant. The make-to-order, repetitive, or batch processing could be accommodated with a single software solution. Bull Anger has set-up two different production control systems using TRITON. This was done because the two production processes were totally different from one another. PCBs are primarily a standard product with a fixed bill of materials and are produced in large volumes while the computer systems needed the product configurator modules to facilitate orders. Further, the TRITON system did not need a lot of customization. The strong functionality of the product configurator module of TRITON would allow Bull Angers to configure the products more efficiently and quickly, and thus result in addressing customer requirements faster. Baan had a French version available at that time. This was important to Bull Angers for acceptance of the system by the end-users. Another reason for TRITON being selected was that it was already being marketed by Bull in Europe and the implementation was done by Bull Integris.

Bull Angers is one of the largest sites running live with TRITON in Europe. The implementation was carried out progressively, department by department. The PCBs was the first department to receive TRITON which was implemented in April 1994, followed by high volume products, such as terminals and workstations which were non-configured products. The implementation continued throughout 1995 for software and documentation products and finally, the complex configured products like computer systems.

With the TRITON system, information can be shared all over the company. This is a significant feature of the system as earlier, the sharing of information was extremely time consuming and sometimes impossible. Bull Anger has definitely benefited from the fully integrated system. Today, orders are processed within 24 hours.

With the savings achieved over the old system, they have been able to fully finance the migration and acquisition of the TRITON system even allowing for the fact that implementation took 18 months instead of the originally planned 12 months.

The TRITON system not only saved costs but also saved time. The administration time was reduced.

With increased competition in the market place, Bull Angers is facing the competition head on. The plant is receiving more and more orders and handling them more efficiently, thus bringing costs down. Bull Angers has now positioned itself as a leading computer system provider.

TWENTIETH CENTURY COMPANIES, INC.

Twentieth Century Companies, Inc. knows what it's like for a company to expand its employee base and its product offerings, and acquire another firm in a few short years. It also knows how critical it is for a company's information systems to keep pace with its growth.

With $45 billion in assets under its management and 62 funds spread over nine investment companies, Twentieth Century is the USA's fourth largest direct-marketed no-load mutual fund complex. In 1987 with 300 employees on the roster, the Kansas city financial institution relied on an internally developed, IBM mainframe-based system. Now, after years of growth and a major acquisition, Twentieth Century's system tracks 2200 employees at several different locations.

Their old system was basically nothing more than a name-and-address-storer. They had bought little PC-based packages for salary management, recruitment, job descriptions, and so forth which grew up around the main-frame system. None of them talked to each other. The information needed was in two different systems, and it became a nightmare to extract the information or run reports from one and combine with other. As an OS/2 shop, their PCs were OS/2-based and they looked at a lot of other vendors with OS/2 clients and finally decided on PeopleSoft for its functionality.

PeopleSoft's solutions also made their recent acquisition of the Benham Capital Management Group much smoother. There is a lot of personnel movement from one location to another and being a dynamic organization their HR has to manage multiple sites. The system enabled them to keep better track of where people are, where they are going, and where they have been.

They were able to meet their customers' needs much more efficiently. In addition to eliminating some paper-based processes, they have also been able to eliminate duplicate entries and redundant systems. They find that PeopleSoft enables them to get information on demand and they have been able to transform data into information.

AMERITECH

Ameritech's divestiture from AT&T in the mid-1980s catapulted the Chicago-based telecommunications giant into new markets. Competition in these markets, namely, cellular, fiber optics, wireless, interactive video is fierce and market pressures are tremendous. Ameritech knew it could meet the challenge. It also knew that, to succeed, it had to change its computing infrastructure.

For years, Ameritech had relied on an internally developed payroll system built on mainframe architecture. The system included some human resources functionality, and it worked-after a fashion. Throughout the company they had convoluted systems and interfaces. In payroll, for example, when an employee left one of their five operating units to work in another, they would have to fire them from the first unit and hire them in the second. The payroll costs were high and they realized that they would never achieve anything without adopting an integrated HR and payroll system. The HR department put their heads together to integrate Ameritech's human resources and payroll systems, and after an extensive evaluation of several vendors, Ameritech selected the PeopleSoft solution.

PeopleSoft acted as the catalyst to bring all their HR processes into a programme they call the **employee service paradigm (ESP)**. They realized exciting benefits for reengineering HR and payroll under the ESP program. The interaction between departments has been very effective and they are serving their employees better than before.

Ameritech is looking forward to using PeopleSoft's position management to match open positions with appropriate employee skills throughout the organization. Position management will also provide Ameritech with data for forecasting and planning. Ameritech business units looking to consolidate service centres can use position management to streamline the administrative processes that will support the new service centres.

Eventually, Ameritech expects to achieve significant savings in systems, payroll, and benefits by streamlining its business processes with PeopleSoft. The Ameritech team has masterfully handled a really large project that's delivering significant benefits. They are good to their people, work well with their business partners, and maintain very high standards while driving change that streamlines their business and improves their processes.

ESSAR STEEL

With an investment of Rs 20 crore, CIO claims payback will be within one year. In what is probably one of the largest ERP projects in India, Essar Steel is spending a whopping Rs 20 crore on its SAP R/3 implementation and other IT and consultancy requirement.

To produce high quality steel with the best ingredients, the company felt the need for an integrated and live information system. Consequently, this project was envisaged and driven by the top management.

Essar has signed up with SAP for a 1000-user license to begin with, and this number is expected to go up to 2000 to 2500 users within a few years. These users would be spread over twenty sites. Already there are 600 users working on SAP at Essar Steel. With this upcoming SAP implementation, the modules that will be automated at Essar Steel will be finance, asset management, product planning, plant maintenance, sales and distribution, quality management control and commitment accounting.

The company also has an in-house developed integrated marketing and product system (IMPS) which handles order entry production planning, quality, dispatches and invoicing. Since this (IMPS) is custom built, it has been integrated into SAP.

Earlier, Essar Steel had also implemented a **payroll/administration and management system (PAMS),** which too will tie in with this SAP implementation. Essar Steel also has other custom built solutions for specific areas. All of these will be dovetailed into the SAP implementation. In fact, even after the full implementation of these three applications only 80 per cent of the company's business requirements would have been met.

Why then did Essar decide to go in for an ERP solution at all? Essar has always deployed the latest technology in every area and the demand for IT services was huge. Specifically, with SAP, they would save on implementation time and would be deploying a proven software which fortune 500 companies use. The benefit arising from the SAP implementation is expected to be tremendous and Essar expects that by the end of 1998, the company's Return-On-Investment (ROI) would be 100 per cent.

Already, at Essar Steel, the lead time for delivery and procurement of materials and products has been shortened which will, in turn, reduce the inventory carrying cost. The other benefits that Essar Steel envisages are transparency and accuracy of data, which will be near 100 per cent. Also, the company can close its books within seven days of the given period closing date and the cost reductions will result in improved bottom lines, and optimization of plant operations in terms of manpower and finance.

JINDAL IRON AND STEEL COMPANY LTD.

The Jindal Group produces MS plates, cold-rolled coils, galvanized coils and sheets.

Jindal has opted for Ramco Marshal for the following reasons:

- It fits with their requirements.
- Jindals have confidence in the vendor.
- It has the latest technology.
- It is a world-class product.

Status of implementation. The phase comprising general ledger, accounts receivables, accounts payable, inventory management systems, purchase order management system, payroll and sales order management systems at all the three locations is live.

The implementation was started in 1995 and it was decided to do so in phases. The first phase comprised financial, logistics HR and payroll activities. The second phase was to cover production, quality control and fixed assets management.

Some of the advantages of going in for Marshal are that the software supported the implementation of the packaged solution without too many changes having to be made in the software and provided competitive advantage to the company by implementing effective and economical IT solutions.

The pitfalls encountered along the route of implementation are:

- Problems were encountered with first version release which took time to stabilize.
- Optimization of procedure took time.
- Bug fixing was needed.
- Bad sizing of hardware.

GODREJ SOAPS AND ASSOCIATE COMPANIES

The group manufactures products like soaps, chemicals, household insecticides, agriculture-based products, animal feeds, edible oils, fruit drinks and its customers include households, chemical industries, and agricultural and livestock companies.

Godrej Soaps, after evaluating various ERP solutions, finally decided on adopting MFG/PRO of QAD Inc. The modules implemented are materials, manufacturing, finance, sales and distribution, costing, MRP, DRP and exports documentation.

The main reasons cited for buying MFG/PRO are:

- Cost effectiveness
- Broad installed base in India
- Fast implementation.

Due to the package and functionality of the solution, there are better controls and seamless information flow. Now all the information is available at one place. This has resulted in accountability and the removal of multiple points of data collection for control and validation resulting in faster and more accurate information. Human checks are no longer required. There is faster and clearer decision-making, better inventory management and equipment utilization resulting in better financial management.

INDIAN RENEWABLE ENERGY DEVELOPMENT AGENCY (IREDA)

IREDA is a financial disbursements company with IS investments till date amounting to three crore rupees yearly. The customers of IREDA are financial intermediaries, direct users, and equipment manufacturers.

IREDA, after closely evaluating various ERP solutions finally decided on IFS. The modules implemented are finance, project monitoring and evaluation, project management, HRM (payroll) and inventory.

Reasons for buying IFS according to the company are that IFS offered strong financial applications in terms of disbursements and repayments of loans and also enabled a certain analysis of project-worthiness and forex risk management. These were best covered by IFS.

The snags encountered in the course of implementation were:

- Attitude of the people
- Multiplicity of processes involved in accomplishing various tasks
- Absence of sufficient knowledge in IT.

ERP HANDLES PRESSURE

SARA ERP CASE STUDY—HAWKINS COOKERS LTD.

Hawkins Cookers Ltd. manufactures pressure cookers and cookware at its plants in Mumbai, Hoshiarpur (Punjab) and Jaunpur (UP). Hawkins is the biggest manufacturer of cookware in India and exports its products to more than 60 countries including the Middle East, Europe, USA, and South-East Asia.

The manufacturing process is discrete manufacturing. A pressure cooker passes through more than 15 shops during which aluminum sheets are converted into pressure cookers. A large number of operations are carried out at subcontractors. Hawkins has multiple product brands, comprising products of various sizes, shapes and models of pressure cookers and kitchenware. It is a household name in India because of its quality products, excellent dealer and service network, and easy availability of spares.

Prior to Sara ERP, Hawkins had a legacy system in Unix and DOS for purchase, store and accounts. Hawkins wanted an integrated system comprising

- Purchase management
- Subcontracting management
- Inventory control
- Accounts payable
- Scrap accounting

- Fixed assets
- Production management (Discrete manufacturing)
- Material requirement planning (MRP)

Since Hawkins has more than 50 subcontractors, it was very important to have a good subcontractor material reconciliation system and precise scrap accounting system. Hawkins' main raw material is aluminum sheets and about 10% scrap is generated from the raw material. This scrap can be sold at about 60% of raw material price.

Hawkins selected Sara-ERP because it trusted that Sara Infotech would customize and implement its system as per their requirement. Implementation started in June 1999 and took around 12 months. It was carried out module by module as per their requirement. The most difficult module to implement at Hawkins was the manufacturing module. It took around six months to create data for operations, norms, and bill of material. The bill of material file itself has approximately 100,000 records in the database. There were different norms for individual, teamwork and group shop (many of them nonlinear) for efficiency calculation of workers.

A WHOLESOME ENTERPRISE APPLICATION

SARA IEMS (ERP III) CASE STUDY—PAN CENTURY OLEOCHEMICALS, MALAYSIA

Pan Century Oleochemical (PCOC) has its factory at Johor Bahru, Malaysia. PCOC manufactures fatty acids, glycerine etc., and exports to more than 50 countries. PCOC has a chemical plant with processes like splitting, fractionation, distillation, hydrogenation and refining glycerine. The main raw material is palm kernel oil and palm stearic oil which are available locally in Malaysia. The raw material, WIP and finished goods are stored in more than 50 storage tanks. The finished goods are sold in flakes, beads and liquid form in drums or in bulk.

PCOC had legacy systems such as Inventory Control, Accounts and Payroll. The company wanted an integrated system comprising Sales, Purchase, Accounts, Manufacturing, Quality Control, Plant Maintenance, etc. PCOC selected Sara-ERP in April 2001. The main reason for selecting Sara-ERP was that it had been successfully implemented at PCOC's group company—Thai Sulphite and Chemicals in Thailand. The implementation of Sara-ERP at PCOC started in May 2001. Sara's consultant carried out the gap analysis. Enhancements and customization were done at the site by a team of three dedicated professionals. It took around nine months to implement the ERP package. The following modules were implemented:

- Sales and invoicing
- Accounts receivables

- Purchase management
- Inventory control
- Accounts payable
- General ledger
- Forex system
- Plant maintenance
- Quality control
- Payroll
- Customer complaint
- Production management
- Raw material planning

PCOC was satisfied with Sara-ERP and further asked Sara to implement Sara-HR at its plant in Malaysia. Sara implemented the following modules of Sara-HR in three months:

- Employee personnel data
- Recruitment and selection
- Manpower planning
- Performance appraisal
- Increment and promotion
- Training
- Medical insurance
- Disciplinary action
- Perks which are part of payroll
- Touring
- Accidents and safety
- MIS reports

After this, PCOC wanted a customized budgeting, costing and business intelligence system to improve business management and reduce waste. These subsystems were customized and implemented in about three months.

PCOC has Decision Control System (DCS), SCADA System, Weight Bridge, Attendance Recording System, Tank Gauging System etc. Sara also provided a seamless integration between the equipment and Sara-ERP.

PCOC has more than 100 users of the system. The database runs on a Sun server and the application runs on an IBM server running Windows 2000. The application database is MS-SQL Server. The clients use Windows NT or Window 98 based PCs to access the ERP.

Appendix

ERPWARE^{TM}—ERP-based Integrated Process Data Business Model

In the conventional organizational set-up, it is very difficult to cut across various departments and meet the supply chain end to end. The gaps between delivery and expectations are critical, and this can be established only with an integrated process data business modelling which considers the various layers of the business and cut across departmental barriers by meeting the supply chain effectively.

The success of any organization today lies in its ability to look at business not as just consisting of strict departmental boundaries but in viewing the entire business as comprising various processes on concentric layers (see Figure A1.1), with each process on a layer having a specific role in bringing competitive advantage to the organization.

The core of any business is data model which consists of entities consisting of internal data and external data and their related attributes. The data model controls the actual data of the entire organization. The first layer, in Figure A1.1 consists of the ERP system which updates the various data that form the database of the enterprise and provide support to the processes in the outer layers in the form of manipulated data, status information, trends, workflow automation and so on.

The second layer comprises the various operating processes which are managed by process owners and not by departmental heads. Each process in this layer extracts data from the ERP system and interacts with other processes in the layer through inter and intra workflow process and then provides data to the ERP system on various transactions.

The third layer consists of the key control processes that take care of the sequencing of the operating processes. The control processes receive status report from the ERP system and provide triggers that are either event-based or time-based as per the sequencing schedule.

The fourth and the outermost layer is the strategic process layer which *collects* information about order winners and qualifiers from the outside environment and creates new processes, *updates* existing processes, and *deletes* those processes which are no longer required. Similarly, they constantly create, delete and update the data model required to support the processes so as to realize the organization's mission, goals and objectives.

Note: ***ERPWARE*** is a registered trade mark of the authors.

Fig. A1.1 Integrated process data business model

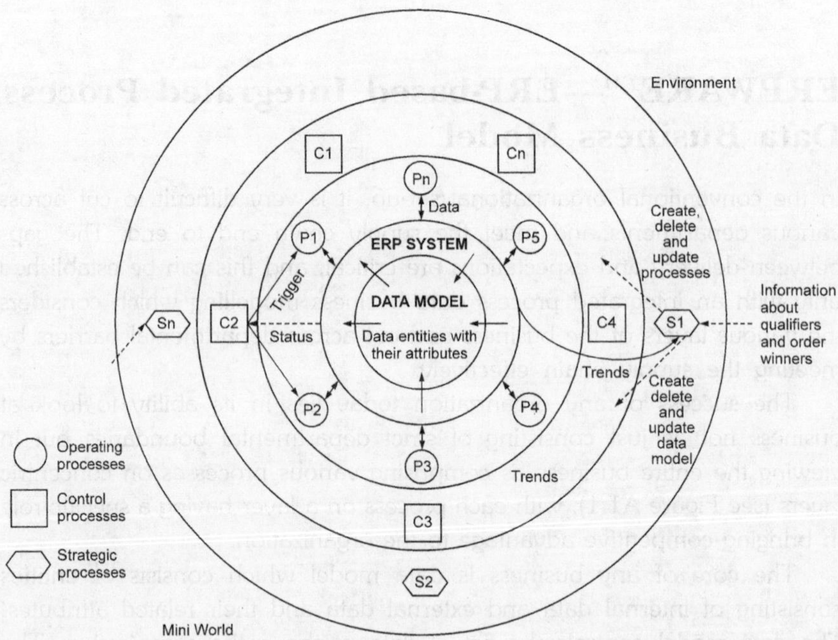

Further Reading

Anshoom Jain, Messing up BIG! *Computer World*, January 1–15, 1998.

ASAP World Consultancy and Jonathan Blain, *Using SAP R/3*. Prentice-Hall of India, New Delhi, 1998.

J. Anandan, Wayward in enterprise maze, *Computers Today*, February 1998.

Jerome Kanter, *Managing with Information*, 4th ed., Prentice-Hall of India, New Delhi, 1996.

L. Subramanyan, Beyond Automation, *Data Quest*, April 15, 1996.

M.V.S. Peri Sastri, Making ERP effective, *Economic Times*, January 30, 1998.

Philip Kotler, *Marketing Management—Analysis, Planning, Implementation and Control*, 11th ed., Prentice-Hall of India, New Delhi, 2001-2002.

Richard Brown, *In search of the total solution*, APICS—The performance advantage, 1995.

Thomas Curran and Gerhard Keller, *SAP R/3 Business Blueprint*, Prentice-Hall PTR, London, 1998.

Vipen Mahajan, 9 steps to success, *Computer World*, January 1–15, 1998.

Vivek Gautam, The modern enterprise paradigm, *Data Quest*, April 1996.

Answers to Selected Problems

CHAPTER 1

1.1 Integrated functionality of an enterprise means the central database shared by all functions of the enterprise, and the ability to share business-critical data more efficiently, both internally and across the extended supply chain. Cross enterprise functionality enables all the departments and divisions in an enterprise not only to share information, but also to work seamlessly with salespeople and suppliers and communicate easily with customers.

The interaction of the enterprise with entities outside it so that it can compete and succeed globally is called **cross enterprise functionality** (see Fig. P1.1).

Fig. P1.1 Cross enterprise functionality

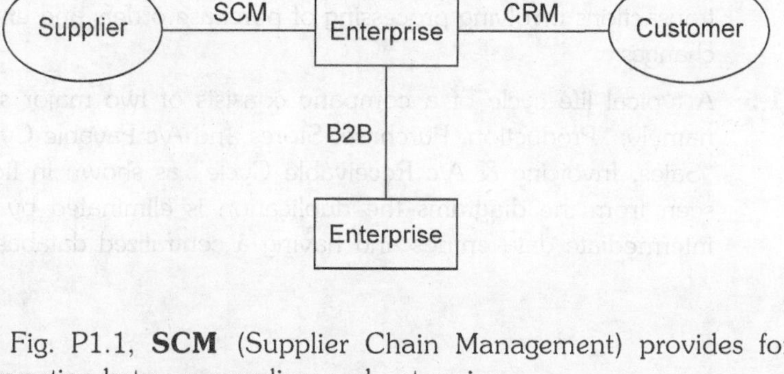

In Fig. P1.1, **SCM** (Supplier Chain Management) provides for interaction between suppliers and enterprise.

CRM (Customer Relationship Management) provides for interaction between enterprise and customer.

Enterprises interact with each other through **B2B** (Business to business integration).

1.2 The various resources that an ERP has to optimize are:

- Human resources
- Equipment
- Time
- Money

These basically constitute the 4 m's (Man, Money, Machines, Materials). Apart from these, information is also a vital resource which needs to be managed and kept up to date.

Methods dealing with optimizing the overall flow of demand and supply data is known as **IRP** (Intelligent Resource Planning). In order to optimize these resources, Intelligent Resource Planning allows an enterprise to build relationship between various activities. This identification of relationship between activities enables one to optimally identify the demand-supply chain. It should include interplant order processing, availability checking, and cost optimization. IRP helps in managing resources by creating alternate scenarios in terms of resource utilization and delivery performance.

1.3 The success of any organization lies in its ability to look at business not as just consisting of strict departmental boundaries, but in viewing the entire business as comprising various processes. The core of any business is data model which consists of entities and their related attributes. The data model controls the actual data of the entire organization.

The heart of any ERP exercise is the creation of an integrated data model. Integrated data model provides support to the processes in the outer layer in the form of manipulating data, status information, trends, workflow automation, and so on. The database reflects transactions involving processing of purchase orders and engineering changes.

1.5 A typical life cycle of a company consists of two major subcycles, namely: “Production, Purchase, Stores and A/c Payable Cycle”, and “Sales, Invoicing & A/c Receivable Cycle” as shown in figures. As seen from the diagrams the duplication is eliminated by avoiding intermediate data entries and having a centralized database.

Fig. P1.2 Production, purchase, stores and A/c payable cycle. Courtesy (Sara Infotech)

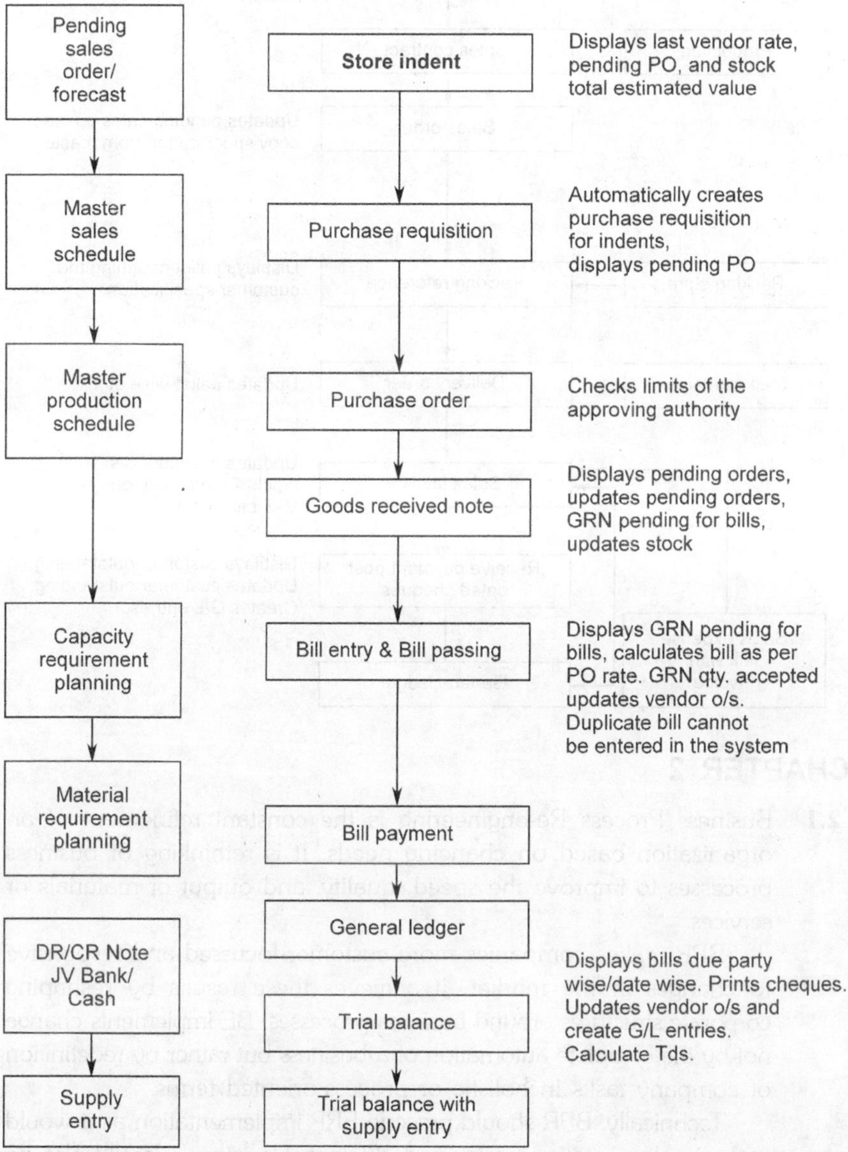

Fig. P1.3 Sales, invoicing and A/c Receivable cycle. Courtesy (Sara Infotech)

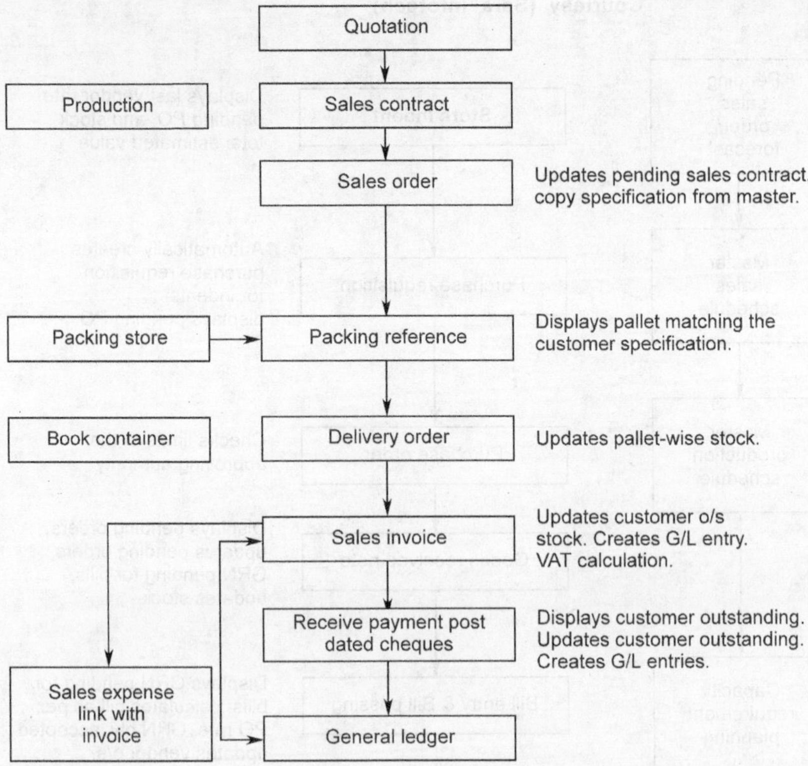

CHAPTER 2

2.1 Business Process Re-engineering is the constant refinement of an organization based on changing needs. It is rethinking of business processes to improve the speed, quality, and output of materials or services.

BPR makes companies more customer-focussed and responsive to changes in the market. It achieves these results by reshaping corporate structures around business processes. BE implements change not by the complete automation of a business but rather by redefinition of company tasks in holistic or process-oriented terms.

Technically, BPR should precede ERP implementation as it would make implementation easier and efficient, However, it could also be taken up simultaneously with implementation. In that case, BPR is referred to as *package enabled re-engineering.*

2.2 In the vast majority of cases, information technology enables BPR. In the past, information technology was used to help companies automate existing business processes but now, technology is being used to change those processes fundamentally, particularly by overcoming constraints existing in manual version of the process.

Today, information technology and business re-engineering go hand in hand. The merger of the two concepts has resulted in the latest concept, namely, business engineering (BE). BE combines the innovations of information technology with BPR's focus on better business processes. The heart and soul of BE lie in radical, process-oriented business solutions, which have been greatly enhanced by the power of information technology. Most of the ERP systems are based on delivering of solution model based on a business engineering blueprint, which represents an advanced integration of business process re-engineering and information technology. We may say ERP enables IT solutions which enable BPR.

3.3 (Please look at Internet, website of ERP package providers, Implementers and Management Consultancy Organizations).

CHAPTER 3

3.1 Example 1

Fig. P3.1 Partial business model for admission of a college student

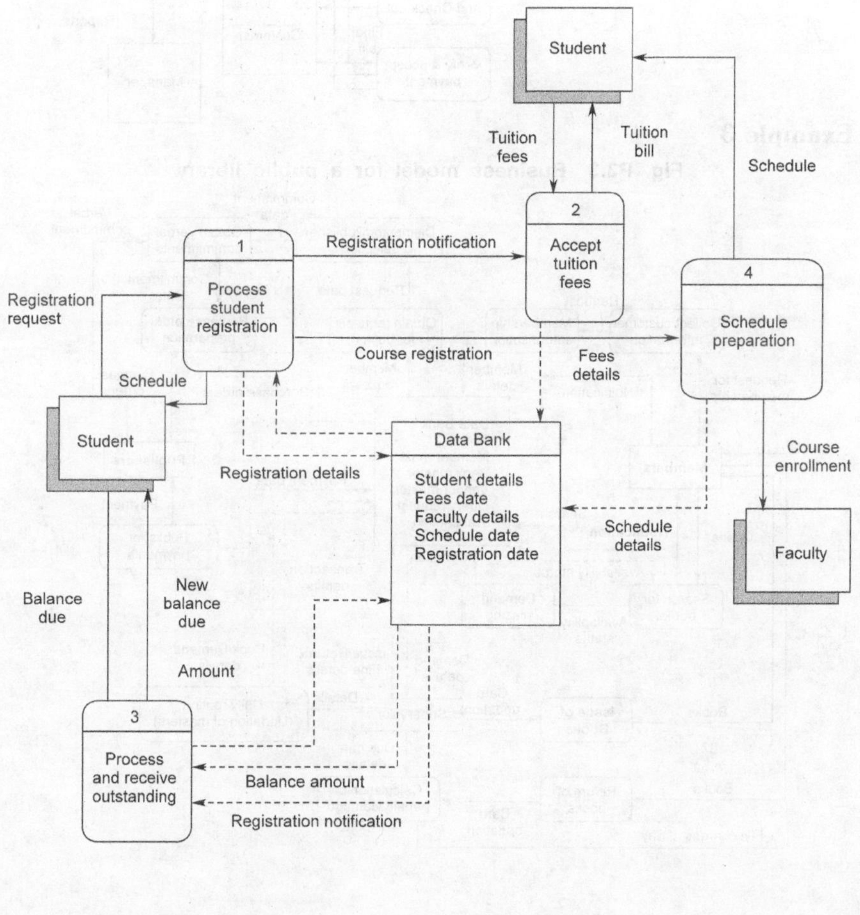

Example 2

Fig. P3.2 Business model for a hotel management system

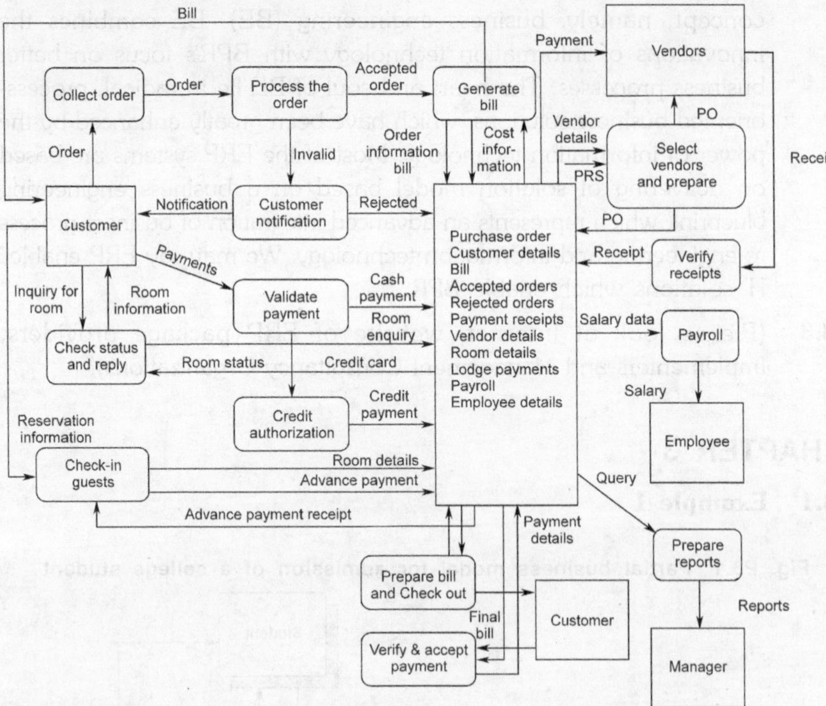

Example 3

Fig. P3.3 Business model for a public library

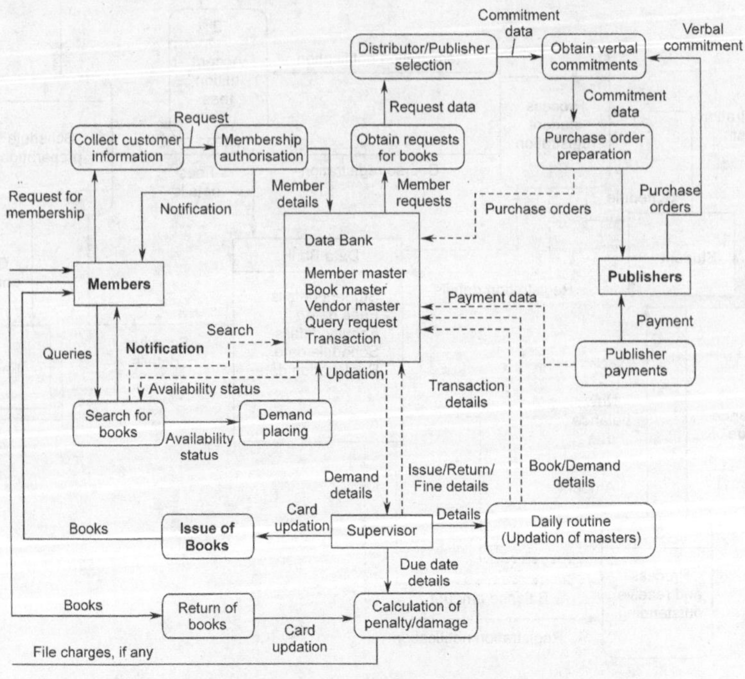

Major Entities and Processes for Public Library

Major Entities

1. Members
2. Vendors
3. Supervisor
4. Books

Major Processes

1. Collect customer information
2. Membership authorization
3. Search for books
4. Demand placing
5. Issue of books
6. Return of books
7. Calculation of penalty/Damage
8. Daily routine
9. Obtain requests for books
10. Publisher/Distributor selection
11. Obtain verbal commitments
12. Purchase order preparation
13. Publisher payments

3.2 The Event-driven Process Chains (EPC) notation is primarily aimed at communicating the business processes in the R/3 Reference Model. The EPC language is targeted to describe processes on the level of their business logic (not necessarily on a formal software specification level) and to be easy to understand and use by business personnel. The methodology inherited its name from the central diagram type that shows the control flow structure of the process as chains of events and functions (see Fig. P3.4).

Fig. P3.4 EPC process diagram

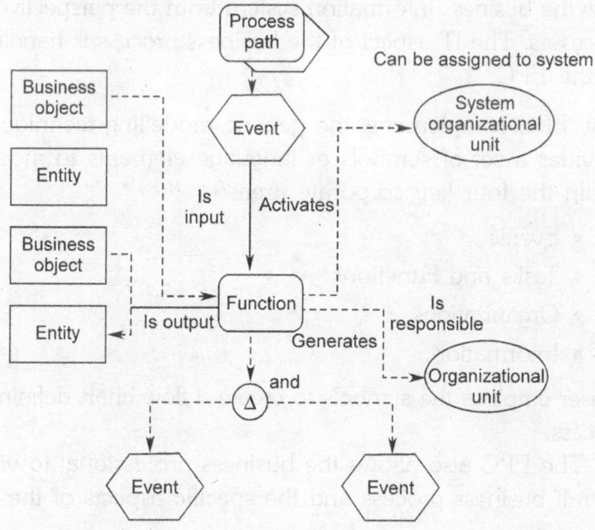

The process language consists of the following elements:

Functions: The basic building blocks are functions. In the context of R/3, they are related to the triggering of transactions on business objects. Extended EPC diagrams additionally show the information being passed in and out of an activity, the required resources as well as the organizational units that are assigned to a function.

Events: Events describe the situation before and after a function is executed, in a semi-formal way. There are internal events, resulting from an activity and external events such as "a customer calls." Naming conventions give hints about the underlying business objects.

Control flow: Links between activities, events and logical operators specify the flow of control.

Logical operation: The above elements can be combined by AND, OR, XOR operators. Implicitly they synchronize parallel threads of execution.

Entity: Entities represent, or model, things in the real world, e.g. sales order, result of check.

Process path: Shows how processes are interrelated.

Organizational unit: Organizational units describe the structure of an enterprise. There are both structural and technical organizational units. An example of an organizational unit is a sales organization.

Business objects: A business object represents something, either real or abstract, in the form of data or components.

The EPC defines a firm as a series of business processes that are triggered by a series of events. The EPC allows a business user to view the business information system from the perspective of business processes. The IT aspect of the business process is handled internally by the EPC.

How EPC complements the generic modelling technique: The EPC provides a set of symbols or language elements to model functions within the four key corporate areas:

- Events
- Tasks and Functions
- Organizations
- Information.

A user employs the symbols to create a flow chart defining a business process.

The EPC also allows the business professional to view both the overall business process and the specific aspects of the process that relate back to the key corporate areas. The Component Model presents the specific tasks executed in the firm's business processes as a hierarchical functional tree. It presents each task and its relationship to other tasks. The Organization Model is like an organizational chart. It illustrates the structure of the firm. The Data Model shows the information that a firm uses and how each discrete piece of information flows from one data unit to the next. Finally, the Interaction Model presents the flow of information among applications and organizational units. Together, the models provide the business professional with a complete picture of the company's business processes in a concise and easy to understand fashion.

CHAPTER 4

4.1 Successful implementation is the obvious goal of any organization that has chosen to go in for enterprise resource planning (ERP). ERP implementation is a special event since it involves the entire organization over a period of time. It brings together different functionality, people, procedures, and ideologies, and leads to sweeping changes throughout the organization.

The steps involved in a total ERP implementation are listed and described on pages 42–46 of the book.

4.2 An ERP package is expected to improve the flow of information and formalize all the business processes and workflow that exist in an organization. As a result, the company starts performing better and in turn benefits the users who have collectively improved their way of working. It is the users who will be driving the implementation, and their active involvement at all levels and across all business functions is absolutely critical.

ERP project team would be charged with the responsibility of implementing the ERP for the specific organization. Ideally, the project team includes members of the IT department, sales, material, manufacturing, plant maintenance and finance. The company also hires an outside consultant from an ERP consulting/implementation partner firm to provide knowledge in the concerned modules and in project management. The IT team must be selected from the best in the company and should comprise those who have the ability to learn the new system.

It is of the greatest importance to form an implementation team consisting of knowledgeable users from all functions, they configure the systems using tables and functions available to run the business in a new way because they are the users of the system and, after implementation, they take responsibility to maintain the system, along with IT personnel and personnel from the implementation consultant. In order to avoid setbacks in an ERP project, a consultant assumes an important role. The job of the consultants, by virtue of their industry, experience and package expertise, is to set the expectations of the users at various levels, keeping in mind the overall business objectives of the client. They can achieve this by working closely with the key users, understanding their needs, analyzing their business realities, and designing solutions that meet the basic objectives of the company.

From the people chosen, the project manager, project leaders and module leaders should be identified and also a steering committee should be formed. A person who is skilled in communication and understands the organization well, should head the ERP team. The leader also must be a person who can keep the motivation level of the implementation team at fairly high levels throughout the several months of implementation.

Thus, though the responsibility of Implementing on ERP package lies with the project team, the responsibility of implementing ERP, i.e. realizing the objectives of implementation lies with senior user Managers. Ownership of an ERP Implementation lies exclusively with the CEO.

4.3 To do ERP right, the ways to do business needs to change and the ways people do their jobs needs to change too.

The important point is not to focus on how long it will take—real transformational ERP efforts usually run between one to three years, on an average—but rather to understand why we need it and how we should use it to improve our business.

While the ERP package implementation ends with system monitoring and fine-tuning, the ERP implementation is an ongoing, continuous process.

Fig. P4.1 Views of business experts on ERP completion

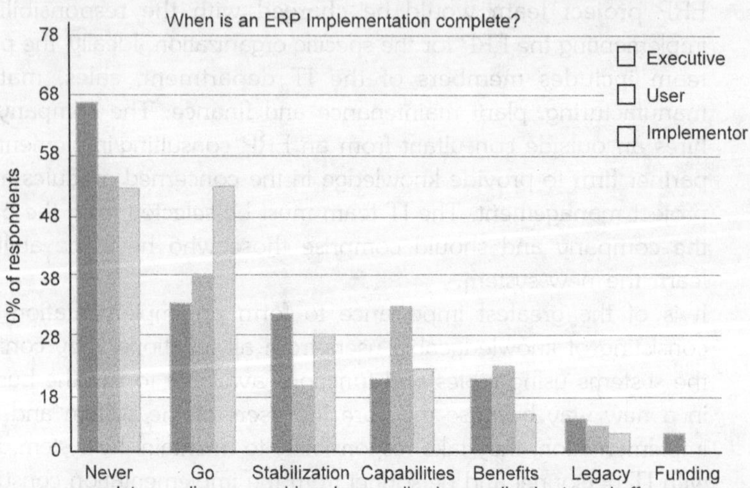

In a study of executives, implementers, and users at companies that have installed an ERP solution, the majority believes that an ERP implementation is never complete. This belief is most strongly held among executives, while the implementers display more of a project mentality.

Post-implementation phase includes:

- Post-live assessment
- Training and documentation supplementation
- Centre of Excellence design and implementation
- Change management and organizational design services
- Knowledge management
- Business process consulting
- Configuration services
- Supply chain management system deployment
- Lean manufacturing consulting and integration

Some organizations use discovery workshops to articulate post-ERP expectations and examine performance metrics, set up as objectives for ERP implementation.

4.4 During the course of ERP implementation, the demand for changing the core package is common. In some cases, it may be impossible to proceed with the overall project without carrying certain alterations. In such a case, it is necessary to customize. Implementation without any customization can leave customers dissatisfied because the ERP project may not meet their requirements. Mass customization can be defined as manufacturing one-of-a-kind product to a customer's exact configuration requirements with the same efficiencies expected for a mass-produced product.

Customizing an ERP package is different from developing a system from scratch due to two main reasons. The first reason is that the space of the feasible requirements in customizing an ERP package of application development is determined by the existing functionality of the package. The second reason is that customer requirements have to be thought of and expressed in terms of the business process models that the package incorporates. The typical scenario of an ERP system customization involves customers who are expected to map the business processes of their own enterprises onto the built-in business processes of the package and based on this mapping to figure out how to configure the functions of the package that support the matched parts of the two processes and how to change the processes of the enterprise that do not have any counterparts in the package. On an average, organizations take about 15.5 months to implement the solution, from start to end, spending almost nine months on the actual implementation and customization. End-user organizations are currently spending as much time customizing their ERP solution as they are on actual implementation.

Case Study of Customization for Second Harvest

EXECUTIVE SUMMARY

Second Harvest is the largest not for profit food charity organization in the US. It distributes over 1.5 billion dollars of food supplies every year to hundreds of food banks and shelter homes across the US. While Second Harvest was implementing ADAGE ERP solution from SCT Corp with the help of one of the big five consulting firms, it was facing acute problems in the area of enterprise reporting. Lack of expertise on the part of the ERP vendor and their implementation partner compelled them to look for someone who could really deliver the solution.

Given below is how i3Connect, Inc. partnered with Second Harvest to deliver quality financial reporting solution and provide management level consulting in the area of ERP customization through smart reports development methodology.

INTRODUCTION

The inability of the existing partners to deliver an appropriate reporting solution worried the management to the extent of considering other ERP systems. It was yet another classic case where the senior management that pays an outrageous sum of money to implement an ERP, only to find out that they can't see an accurate P&L or Balance Sheet coming out of the system! This is when i3Connect, Inc. (formerly known as Intranet 2001, Inc.) was invited to save the project by delivering critical financial reports and to train some of the client's resources to carry on the task in the future.

CHALLENGE

The ERP solution that Second Harvest had implemented did not come with the usable library of working reports. The ERP vendor and other partners that worked with Second Harvest did not provide much expertise in this area. Visibility to critical business parameters was being hampered because of poor reporting capabilities. What Second Harvest needed was the team of strong professionals who understood Adage ERP, who offered strong business functional skills, and had a proven track record and methodology to deliver customized financial reporting solution. i3Connect, Inc. offered exactly what they needed. At the same time Second Harvest realized that in order to develop these skills in house to carry on their multisite rollout, they needed a partner who could share their working methodology and train their own resources with the long-term view in mind.

i3Connect, Inc. offered proven capabilities in the area of ERP customization through smart reporting. They had their own "Information Retrieval" methodology which was offered to Second Harvest to build financial reporting solution. They delivered the solution through the following steps:

1. In the situation the client was, they first attacked the most critical areas of enterprise reporting that their partners had tried and could not deliver and followed a two-pronged approach where we worked on critical deliverables, first while working with their existing partners to train their resources to support the rollout.
2. Developed set of critical financial reports to match requirement using their i3Connect framework. Their drive has always been to prevent the client solution from getting trapped in proprietary tool sets. They always try to make the solution as free and as open as possible from the proprietary tools. Hence, they custom programmed financial reporting knowledge and business rules in SQL stored procedures that wrote their intermediate and final results on relational data tables. Report templates simply queried these tables and formatted the data as per the design. However, no business rules existed in these report templates.
3. This design would allow Second Harvest in the future to change their relational database technology and also if they so wished, to upgrade to a better reporting tool. Their investment in the solution will stay intact as all business rules were coded in SQL, which is an industry standard language and supported across databases and tools.

DISADVANTAGES OF OVERCUSTOMIZATION

Customization is costly, time consuming and, very often, impractical. This leads to a situation in which the organization must change many of its work processes and adapt to the ERP program rather than the other way around. Whenever the processes represented in the ERP software differ significantly from the processes used by the firm, one has two options. The first is to build the organizational process into the ERP software through customization. The second one is to change the practice followed by the firm to suit the process native to the ERP software. Traditional common sense would force people to customize the software to suit the individual demands of the organization.

This leads to two problems. The first reason arises from the fact that any customization done locally is outside the core ERP software. Accordingly, the next release of the ERP software would not support local customization. They have to be redone by the end user for the new release. Second, the very purpose of ERP is to take advantage of the best practices in industry that come embedded with the ERP software. By overcustomizing the implementers would deprive the benefit of world-class practice to the organization that is implementing ERP. The way to bring ERP projects in on time and on budget is to keep customization to a minimum, according to Information Week. Some analysts believe that the long lead times required by ERP implementation are driving a shift to postproduction ERP customization. Although minimizing customization results in "vanilla ERP," vendors are increasingly bringing out software with features and functions that meet a range of needs.

4.5 (Selecting an ERP solution is part of an overall IT strategy. The IT strategy should be derived from overall Business or Corporate Strategy. In some cases IT strategy forms an important component of Corporate Strategy.)

4.6 The most common problems faced during ERP implementation are:

- Need for customization
- Inadequate training resources
- Lack of support from management

Other problems identified as being associated with ERP implementation include the following:

(i) Enormous technical challenges of rolling out ERP systems which are complex pieces of software that require large investments of money, time and expertise to install.

(ii) Failure to reconcile the technological imperatives of the ERP system with the needs of the business. (*Note:* An enterprise system imposes its own logic on a company's strategy, organization and culture).

(iii) Pushing companies towards full integration even when a certain degree of business unit segregation may be in its best interest.

(iv) Pushing companies towards generic processes even when customized processes may be in its best interest.

(v) Conflicts between the system logic may conflict with the logic of the business which may result in a failed implementation or a weakening of the company's important sources of competitive advantage.

(vi) Convergence around a single software and similar processes by members of the same industry raises questions regarding how competitive advantage can be maintained;

(vii) High costs associated with customizing ERP systems when the ERP system and company strategy clash.

(viii) Companies installing enterprise systems having to adapt or completely rework their processes in order to fit the requirements of the system.

CHAPTER 5

5.1 *Competitive advantage* is the significant contribution to the overall success to the business. This aims at responding to the corporate demands and expectations by undertaking currently popular solutions and modelling operations on best practice to achieve an edge over the other qualifiers to be successful order winners. Earl's procedure for gaining competitive advantage is given in Fig. P5.1.

Fig. P5.1 Earl's procedure for gaining competitive advantage

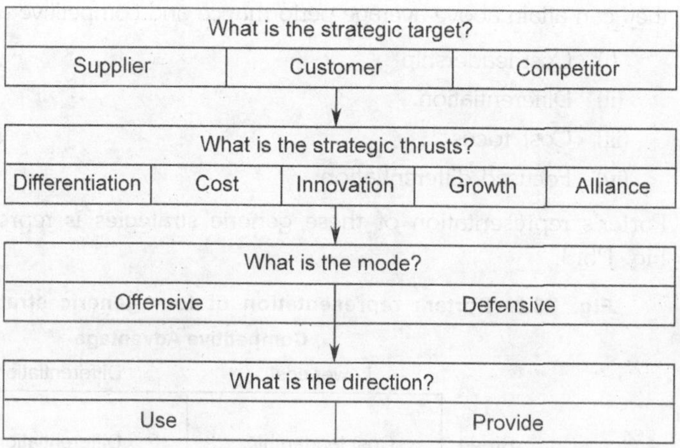

Competition means cultivating unique strengths and capabilities, and defending them against imitation by other firms. Competitive strategy is an enterprise's plan for achieving sustainable competitive advantage over, or reducing the edge of, its adversaries.

Porter's classic diagram representing the key forces, which make up the industry structure, is reproduced in Fig. P5.2.

Fig. P5.2 Forces driving industry competitive

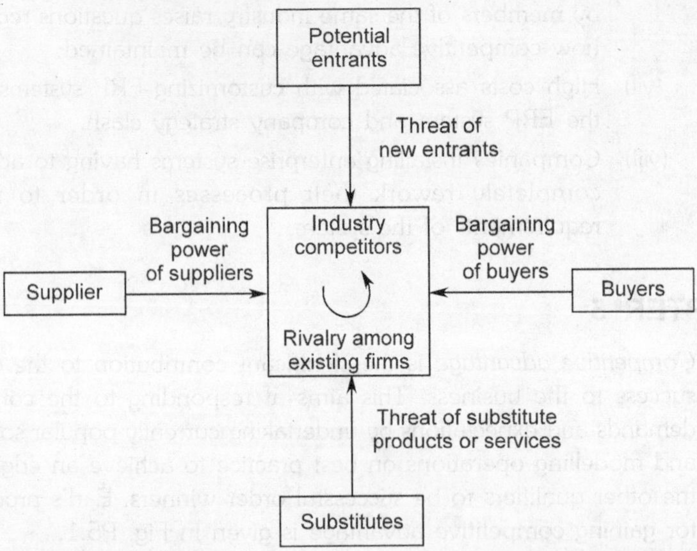

Enterprises have four generic strategies available to them whereby they can attain above-average performance and competitive advantage.

(i) Cost leadership
(ii) Differentiation
(iii) Cost focus
(iv) Focused differentiation.

Porter's representation of these generic strategies is reproduced in Fig. P5.3.

Fig. P5.3 Porters representation of four generic strategies

		Competitive Advantage	
		Lower cost	Differentiation
Competitive scope	Broad target	Cost leadership	Differentiation
	Narrow target	Cost Focus	Focused differentiation

Competitive advantage grows out of the way an enterprise organises and performs discrete activities. To gain competitive advantage over its rivals, a firm must either provide comparable value to the customer, but perform activities more efficiently than its competitors (lower cost), or perform activities in a unique way that creates greater buyer value and commands a premium price (differentiation).

Many **differentiation bases** exist, classified into four major groups:

(i) Product (quality, features, options, style, brand name, packaging, sizes, services, warranties, returns)

(ii) Price (list, discounts, allowances, payment period, credit terms)

(iii) Place (channels, coverage, locations, inventory, transport)

(iv) Promotion (advertising, personal selling, sales promotion, publicity).

It can be used to support or sharpen the firm's product through these various attributes. The activities performed by a particular enterprise can be analysed into primary activities, which directly add value to the enterprise's factors of production, which are together referred to as the *value chain*, and supporting activities.

The primary, value-adding activities include those involved in the production, marketing delivery, and servicing of the product. They are linked, generally, in a chain. Support activities include those providing purchased inputs, technology, human resources, or overall infrastructure functions to support the primary activities.

By coordinating linked activities, an enterprise can reduce transaction costs, gather better information for control purposes, and substitute less costly operations in one activity for more costly ones elsewhere. Coordinating linked activities is also an important way to reduce the combined time required to perform them. Hence coordination is increasingly important to competitive advantage. Gaining competitive advantage requires that an enterprise's value chain be managed as a system rather than as a collection of separate parts. Reconfiguring the value chain, by re-locating, re-ordering, re-grouping, or even eliminating activities is often at the root of major improvement in competitive position.

Competitive advantage is a function of how well a company can manage the entire industry value-chain. A corporation can create competitive advantage by coordinating its links in that chain.

5.2 The advent of ERP has brought about an organized approach to managing order-winners and qualifiers as they need an integrated perspective to do so. ERP has tried to handle this process by providing answers to the following questions:

(i) What information do we need to manage the order-winners and qualifiers and what data model is required to support it?

(ii) How can groupware, workflow and document management technology be integrated to improve communication among work groups, manage paper documents by routing them electronically, and control data so as to enable organizational processes to realize relevant order-winners and qualifiers?

- ERP has also helped organizations realize order-winners and qualifiers by providing a software that facilitates modelling of logistic processes in terms of items, bill of materials, routing and also registering the goods flow in the processes in terms of production order and inventory. Support for making decisions based on logistic processes is built into these packages today. The intelligent resource planning, which is built into many of these packages, provides advanced material and capacity planning facilities so as to take care of order-winners and qualifiers in a specific situation.

5.3 (Look at websites of ERP product suppliers, Implementation solution providers and management consultancy organizations)

CHAPTER 6

6.2 Most of the industrial enterprise applications market revenue is generated by application software license sales, with enterprise resource planning (ERP) software leading at 35% market share. ERP is followed by mechanical CAD/CAE/CAM at 34% and plant operations at 13%. ERP is expected to strengthen its hold on the market and will likely increase its market share from 35% to nearly 46% by 2001. Much of ERP 's market growth is driven by an increasingly global business focus.

Historically, the enterprise applications market has been supported by Fortune 500 companies with incomes from $250 million to more than $1 billion. Today, these companies represent 65% of software revenues. Vendors are realizing, however, that there is a largely untapped market of mid-sized companies with incomes between $50 million and $250 million. The customer base for the industrial enterprise applications market is also shifting in terms of geography. For example, while North America and Europe still hold the largest market shares (48% and 33%, respectively), Asia/Pacific, Latin/South America and Africa are expected to be the new lands of opportunity. Steady growth is expected in these areas over the next several years.

ERP vendors in particular are beginning to reach out to customers by opening industry expertise centres for their most promising vertical markets. Vendors across the market are also forming an increasing number of partnerships with industry-specific point tool vendors to develop product features that satisfy the industry-specific needs of their customers. The global ERP market is expected to grow to about

20 billion USD by the turn of the century from its present level of about 7 billion dollars. In future, more and more of the installations are likely to use industry specific solutions.

The Indian ERP market is around 1000 crores and growing at the healthy 30% annual growth. All the leading industrial houses are getting their act of ERP implementation together. There will be a major ERP implementation exercise by the public sector corporations in the next few years.

All the key players in the ERP global market are practically present in India. This includes SAP with their flagship product R/3, Baan Company with their Baan IV product, Oracle with their Oracle Applications, and the world-class ERP Product *Marshall* from the rising Indian star Ramco Systems. Yet another leading product MFG/ PRO from QAD has been present for a while (the two customers Hindustan Lever & Godrej have been using it for over two years). SAP has been exceptionally successful in India with nearly two-thirds of the Indian market share. The major industrial houses Tata, Reliance, Essar, Mahindra & Kirloskar have embraced SAP. Baan has been very successful in major manufacturing companies such as TVS. Oracle has been playing a dominant role in the telecom centre with a stronghold among all cellular phone companies.

6.3 (A sample presentation Outline is given in Fig. P6.1 for guidance purposes.)

Fig. P6.1

ENTERPRISE RESOURCE PLANNING

The Only Permanent Thing is "Change"

- Winners
- ↗ Gather Crucial Information
- ↗ Quick Action
- ↗ Get Competitive Advantage

Fig. P6.1 (cont.)

WHY ERP

- A "Total" Solution
- Traditional Approach:
  - Islands of Information
  - Lack of Integration
  - Difficult Data Consolidation
  - Difficulty in Managerial Control

BENEFITS OF ERP

- Better Customer Satisfaction
- Improved Vendor Performance
- Increased Flexibility
- Reduced Quality Cost
- Improved Resource Utility
- Improved Information Accuracy & Integrity
- Improved Decision-Making Capability
- Best Business Practices in the World
- Better Solution in terms of E-Commerce

Fig. P6.1 (cont.)

SCOPE OF ERP

- **Financials:**
  - Financial Accounting
  - Treasury Management
  - Enterprise Control
  - Asset Management
- **Logistics:**
  - Production Planning
  - Materials Management
  - Plant Maintenance
  - Quality Management
  - Project Systems
  - Sales & Distribution
- **Human Resources:**
  - Personnel Management
  - Training & Development
  - Skill Inventory
- **Work Flow:**
  - Flexible Assignment of Tasks & Responsibilities

RISKS IN ERP

- Changed Business Processes
- Hurried Implementation
- User Adaptation
- High Time & Money Investment

"ERP Does Not Ensure Success in Business"

Fig. P6.1 (cont.)

SCOPE FOR OUTSOURCING

- Affordability
- Include Software Customization
- Integration with Other Back-end Systems
- Ongoing Maintenance of the Applications

ERP PACKAGES

- SAP
- Oracle
- JD Edwards
- Peoplesoft
- Baan
- SSA (Systems Software Associates
- Indian Products

CHAPTER 7

7.2 (A sample outline only for example purpose)

Fig. P7.1

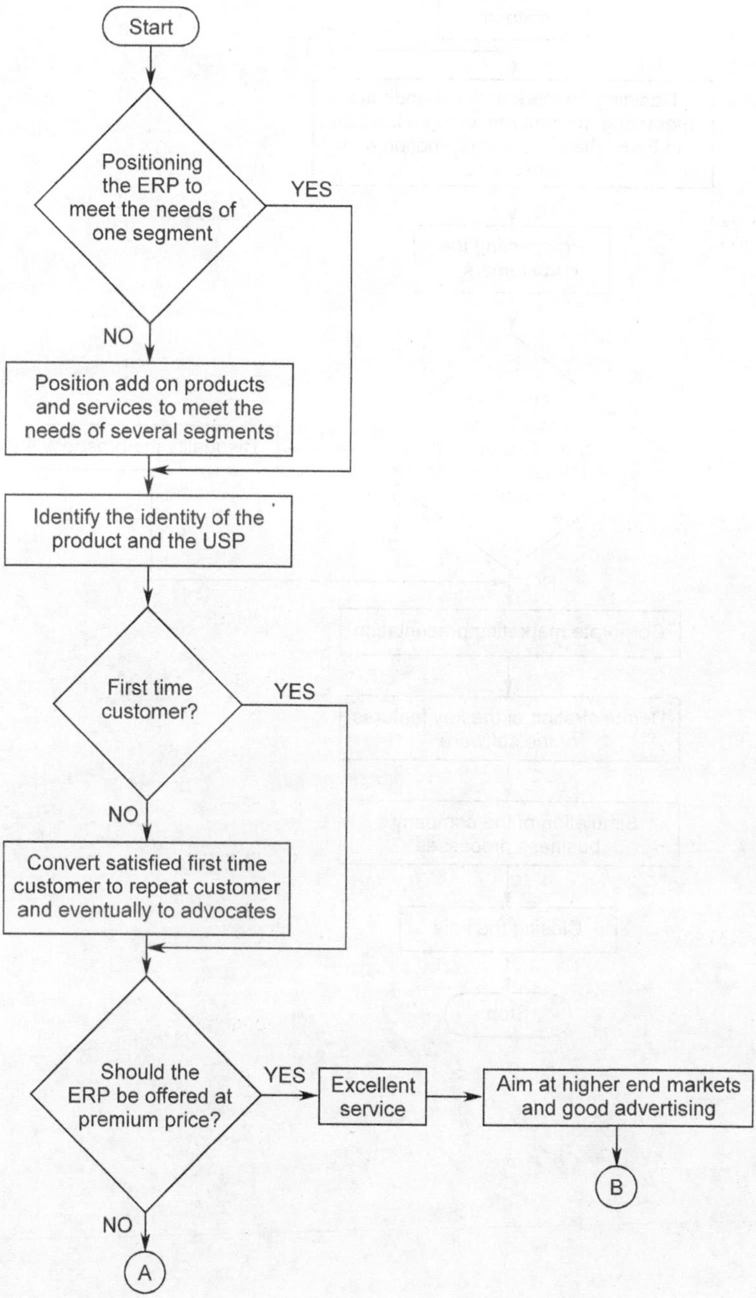

Fig. P7.2

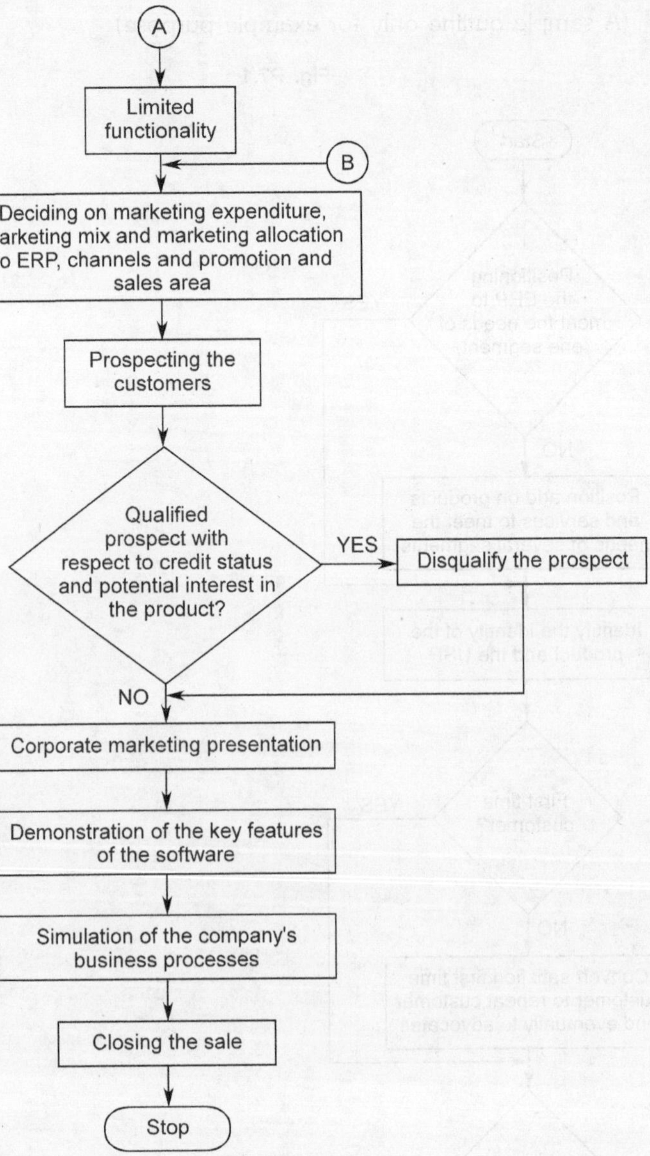
A
Limited functionality
B
Deciding on marketing expenditure, marketing mix and marketing allocation to ERP, channels and promotion and sales area
Prospecting the customers
Qualified prospect with respect to credit status and potential interest in the product?
YES
Disqualify the prospect
NO
Corporate marketing presentation
Demonstration of the key features of the software
Simulation of the company's business processes
Closing the sale
Stop

Index